building family ties

with
faith, love & laughter

DAVE STONE

THOMAS NELSON
Since 1798

NASHVILLE   DALLAS   MEXICO CITY   RIO DE JANEIRO

Building Family Ties with Faith, Love & Laughter

© 2012 by Dave Stone

Published in Nashville, Tennessee, by Thomas Nelson®. Thomas Nelson is a registered trademark of Thomas Nelson, Inc.

Designed by Thinkpen Design.

The "FAMILY" photo which appears on page 11 was provided by Carmella Calhoun and used with permission.

Thomas Nelson, Inc., titles may be purchased in bulk for educational, business, fund-raising, or sales promotional use. For information, please e-mail SpecialMarkets@ThomasNelson.com.

ISBN-13: 978-1-4003-2255-8

Printed in China

12 13 14 15 16 [RRD] 5 4 3 2 1

www.thomasnelson.com

Dedication

This book is dedicated to the three
most joyful kids in the world—

Savannah, Sadie, and Sam.

Anyone who's around you always comments
on your faith, selflessness, and joy. You
brighten my day. You make parenting fun.
The memories recounted in this book don't
begin to scratch the surface of countless
others that bring an instant smile to my face.

Thanks for the joy you bring. Mom
and I are the most blessed parents in
the world—all because of you.

Love,

Dad

Acknowledgments

To my wife, Beth: your wisdom scattered throughout this book will bless so many. Thanks for graciously putting up with me during these hectic months, and for your constant encouragement and perseverance. We survived the stress of writing a book—maybe now we're ready to wallpaper a room together!

Thanks to Sam and Gwen Stone for modeling how to build family ties through faith, love, and laughter. Those words are a great description of the home in which you raised me.

To the best brother in the world, Jeff Stone. I hope the stories in here bring back fond and fun memories. You are the greatest and most encouraging pastor I know.

This book became a labor of love thanks in part to a multitude of friends who allowed me to bounce my ideas off of them. So thanks to my team of encouragers and readers who invested in this project because of their love for the family. They are: Sara Burke, Carl and Lindsay Kuhl, Tish Cordrey, Kisa Hoeltke, Karissa Sites, Mary Leslie, Rebecca St. James, and Jeff Stone.

Thanks to Michael Howerton for providing a place free from interruptions and just fifteen minutes away!

Thanks to my writing coach, Penny Stokes, for making my ground beef seem like filet mignon. You are a great teammate!

Thanks to my *family* at Thomas Nelson: Laura Minchew, Lisa Stilwell, Jack Countryman, Jennifer Deshler, and Michael Aulisio.

Table of Contents

1

Endangered Species

ave you ever spent time browsing the endangered species list? It's fascinating. Worldwide there are currently more than 10,000 animals and 9000 plants in danger of extinction. On that list you'll find everything from Abbott's booby to Zuniga's dark rice rat. You'll find epauletted fruit bats and splayfoot salamanders, skinks and corals, viperous toads and brush-tailed wallabies.

There's one species, however, that inadvertently got left off the list: the joyful Christian family.

Is it just me, or do you see the distractions and diversions of this world sucking the life out of families? In a world of electronic devices, hectic schedules, and temptation at every turn, the family is suffering. As someone once said, "If Satan can't make you bad, he'll keep you busy"—and he has.

So many pressures compete for our time and energy these days. Technology that should free us, instead, seems to absorb our attention like a black hole. Stuff that used to be entertaining, like sports, music, and other extracurricular activities, has turned into duties drained of excitement and spirit. We're so exhausted that we drag ourselves through our days, fall into bed, and then get up the next morning and do it all over again.

We don't have fun anymore. Delight has been deleted. Joy and fulfillment have been replaced by worry and hurry.

It's no wonder that the joyful Christian family has become all but extinct.

The Journey to Joy

Would you like to rediscover a life of joy and contentment, where your home is the center and your family actually enjoys being together? Then press the "pause" button, have a seat, and let's explore the way back.

Last year my wife, Beth, and I attended a conference for pastors and their spouses. The event was held at a very nice resort—chocolates on the pillows at night and towels folded in animal shapes. This was not some shabby motel.

Throughout our stay I was intrigued by the name badges each employee wore. All the badges had the employee's name, of course, but below that was not their hometown or their department at the resort. Instead, there was the word *Passion*.

Some of the "passions" listed were predictable: *golf, travel, music*. One jovial worker listed *food* as his passion, and no one seemed to doubt his honesty. The novelty of the name badges generated a lot of conversation during that week.

On our last day, out of curiosity, I asked the manager, "What's the most prevalent passion your employees list?"

Without hesitation, he responded, "Family."

Most folks would claim that family is their number one priority. Why, then, don't more children feel important to their parents? Why don't families spend time together? Why is everybody going in different directions? What happened to the fun?

Think about it. Jesus said, "I have come that they may have life, and have it to the full" (John 10:10). Life to the full—or, as another translation puts it, "life abundantly."

If that's God's priority, shouldn't it be ours as well? Don't you long for it?

So if Jesus spoke of full, abundant living, and if we all love our families, then shouldn't that be a winning combination (of two ingredients) that's better than a Reese's cup?

And shouldn't abundant life begin at home, with the people you love and cherish the most?

Truth is, a joyful Christian family is pretty much like chocolate and peanut butter. It's addictive. It's delicious.

And it's possible.

Finding the Fun Again

D o you know what an oxymoron is? It's a common phrase that contains an inherent contradiction: *jumbo shrimp, organized chaos, obvious secret, harmless lie, easy childbirth.*

Members of my church might add *short sermon* . . .

But let me suggest another oxymoron—*joyless Christian.*

I remember seeing a T-shirt once: "If Jesus is in your heart, then please notify your face!" (I wanted that to be the title of this book. It didn't happen.)

But the message of the shirt is true. If Christ dwells in us, then we should be distinct from the world, especially when it comes to joy.

A normal week for me involves being a husband to Beth and father to three, leading a staff of 400 and writing a sermon to preach to more than 20,000 people. I am invited to countless meetings, functions, services, and parties each year. Such demands are exhilarating, but they're also dangerous. We've had to be vigilant about protecting our family time.

Now, my family would tell you that they are more important to me than my job. But it wasn't always like that, and it didn't happen by accident.

We've had to carve out Friday family nights, date nights, game nights, family vacations, track meets, baseball games, and countless late-night parties with teens in our home. There is purpose behind our planning and activities. We work at it.

And while Beth and I have made plenty of mistakes in parenting three children, by God's grace each of our children has genuine joy. We laugh a lot.

And why shouldn't we? Christians ought to have more joy than anyone else. We ought to be known as the party animals of the world. Folks should be beating a path to our doors to learn how to have fun.

We've got all kinds of reasons to be joyful. Christ has taken up residence in our hearts. Jesus has made it possible for us to live after we die. The Spirit of God lives within us. Those assurances should radically affect the way we approach and appreciate each day.

I hope you agree with my logic. Jesus does. (How's that for playing a trump card early on?)

He really does, remember? "I have come that they may have life, and have it to the full" (John 10:10). You can't add anything to full to make it *fuller*. That's as good as it gets!

Our day-to-day attitudes with our families grow out of an internal relationship with Jesus, not the external circumstances of life. And so no matter what happens *to* us, abundant life is what happens *in* us—unbridled joy. Family unity. Fun times. Close relationships.

And laughter. Lots and lots of laughter.

Fact or Fiction?

Maybe you're wondering: *Can a family truly find joy together in a culture that seems intent on undermining it? Even my family?*

Listen to the promise one more time: "I have come that you may have life to the full."

That promise comes straight from the One who created you in His image.

Some of you are new parents who want to start your family off on a different pathway than some of the disheartening examples you've observed or experienced. Some of you want to elevate the expectation of joy within your home and enhance the level of communication and connection. And others may need a complete makeover.

God specializes in new beginnings and second chances.

So, how do you generate genuine joy in your family? Well, you certainly don't do it by acting like it's already there. If you're merely interested in the perception that others have of you, then go audit a drama class at your local community college.

We're not interested in simply *appearing* to be happier than others. We want the real thing. If you long to have a joyful family, to delight in your time together, to like one another as well as love one another, then this book was written with you in mind.

On these pages, you'll learn how to develop a family mission statement. I'll teach you how to make lasting memories out of everyday outings and mealtimes. After a while it will become second nature for you to seize teachable moments and do spontaneous things with your family.

This book will show you how to find meaning in the madness. It will help you learn how to protect your family time and take pleasure in one another's company. You'll come to understand the difference between happiness and joy and why your family should pursue true joy—and expect to experience it.

Here's the secret nobody's told you yet: you can have the fun I've been describing and still be a family of individuals with living, active faith.

- Siblings can get along.
- Teens can appreciate time with their parents.
- Dinnertime can be the highlight of the day.
- The three-hour drive to Grandma's house can be enjoyable even without a DVD player—or anything that begins with the letter *i*.
- Secrets and sullenness can be replaced by shared struggles.
- Scowls can be transformed to smiles, grunts to belly laughs, and selfishness to service.

Anyone interested?

Famous Last Words

I've spent countless hours visiting in hospital rooms, and I've come to realize that when people are dying, their conversations are usually brutally honest and free of pretense. You name it, I've heard it—doubts, regrets, lost dreams, unfulfilled desires.

But I've never known anyone who lamented, "I spent *too much* time with my family."

At the end, we all know what's really important. When you're on the threshold between this life and the next, looking across into eternity, don't you want to be surrounded by a family that is tied together with genuine love, faith, and the memories of a great life together?

Come to think about it, don't you want that *now*?

Is your family on the endangered species list? Many families today are. You don't need to read a book to raise kids who are aimless, joyless, and Christless. Simply get in line and follow the crowd.

But if you want your family to be different from the world and if you want to break the unhealthy habits you've grown up with and start building a healthy, joyful, godly family, you will need a book. It's called the Bible.

Join me as we spend the rest of *this* book applying the principles from *that* book.

Prepare to be challenged to get out of your comfort zone and establish a home where everyone enjoys one another.

Together let's build family ties with faith, love, and laughter.

2

Which Way from Here?

Remember *Alice's Adventures in Wonderland*, when Alice came upon the Cheshire Cat sitting in the crook of a tree?

"Would you tell me, please, which way I ought to go from here?"

"That depends a good deal on where you want to get to," said the cat.

"I don't much care where—" said Alice.

"Then it doesn't matter which way you go," said the cat.

"—so long as I get somewhere," Alice added as an explanation.

"Oh, you're sure to do that," said the cat, "if you only walk long enough."[1]

Wise cat.

Often we feel like Alice, standing at a fork in the road, looking in both directions, not knowing which way to go.

The Cheshire Cat's response offers us a profound and troubling truth: If you don't know where you're going, any road will do. And if you keep on, in no particular direction, you're sure to get *somewhere*—but don't be surprised if it's not the place you hoped for.

What's your goal for your family? You may be thinking, *That's simple—survival. Each night when my head touches the pillow, I'm just thankful I made it through another day.*

Sometimes survival seems like the best we can do. But it is, at best, a short-term goal. Let's think a little farther down the road. If your *passion* is your family, what's your *purpose* as a parent? Your answer will determine whether your family experiences frustration or fulfillment.

Look around at the families in your neighborhood. Contrary to popular opinion, the success of a family is not measured by the speed you travel or how many different directions you go. Frantic and frenzied schedules seldom add character or depth to a family.

It reminds me of the old joke about two friends heading off on a road trip to California. As they're speeding along the highway, the passenger asks the driver, "How are we doing?" And his buddy replies, "I have no idea where we are, but we're making great time!"

That's the heart of the problem for many families: lack of direction. Like Alice, they're not sure which way to go, but from the looks of all the activity around them, they need to be going somewhere—and fast. If you don't much care where you're headed, then save yourself fifteen minutes and skip this chapter. Better yet, sell this book on eBay, because if you don't have a purpose, these pages are meaningless.

Determining Your Direction

In the business world, leaders spend a great deal of time and money developing a mission statement. That prime directive becomes the foundational principle for every job in the organization, every decision, every change, every dollar spent. When the mission is understood and embraced, it serves as a compass for every employee. Everyone aims toward that goal, and the company succeeds.

We know it works for business. Why, then, don't we give more attention to the mission of our families? How can we be such fierce and focused leaders at work and not bring the same principles and practices home? A clear vision for the family, repeated and woven into the fabric of daily life, results in joy, direction, and confidence. Rather than aimlessly meandering in a maze, your family can find meaning through its mission.

I can hear you muttering under your breath, "Nobody said anything about homework. Besides, we've gone this long without a family mission statement. What's the big deal about doing it now?"

Here's the big deal. To steal a line from the feline, "If you don't know where you are going, any road will take you there."

Think about it this way: Your phone or car may have a GPS, but until you lock in a destination, all it does is show you where you are. You can't get to where you want to be until you know where you want to go.

Developing a Family Mission Statement

In the first book of the Faithful Families series, we set the goal of *Raising Your Kids to Love the Lord*. We all want that, but let's kick it up another notch. If we truly are serious about *Building Family Ties with Faith, Love & Laughter,* we'll need a compass to get us there. That compass is the family mission statement.

A mission statement is not something parents come up with and then impose on their kids. It's a family project. You need to involve everybody in the process; decide together what your values are and how they can be reflected in your mission. When everyone has a voice, you'll have what the business world calls "buy in" for years to come. Everyone takes ownership. Everyone is invested in the outcome.

It doesn't matter if your children are five or fifteen. A family mission statement provides a rallying point, a focus, a center of gravity that holds your family together.

It doesn't matter if your children are five or fifteen. A family mission statement provides a rallying point, a focus, a center of gravity that holds your family together.

So, how do you go about it? It's a simple process, really.

- Pray for God to give you all clear direction and unity.
- Discuss principles and goals that are important to your family.
- Talk about how you'd like the family to be remembered years from now.
- Write down several possible statements. (See examples that follow.)
- Narrow it down to the best one, then pray about it for several days.
- Reconvene and determine your family mission statement.
- Schedule a regular time for the family to pray and evaluate your progress.

There are lots of creative ways to do this. You might want to brainstorm with your family by getting a large piece of poster board and some brightly colored markers. Place the poster in a prominent spot—near the breakfast table, maybe, or on the side of the refrigerator. For a few days, let everyone in the family write on it—graffiti-style—significant Bible verses, ideas, prayers, fruit of the Spirit, hopes, and wishes for the family. Set a time to brainstorm, agree on the principles, and identify goals that are important for your family. Use those as the basis for your mission statement.

A Few Examples

Relax. This is not a test. There is no right or wrong way to go about it, no grades, no black marks on your permanent record. You are crafting this around the way your family is wired, so *your mission statement will be different from anyone else's.* The detail, length, and intent are up to you.

Kurt and Kristen Sauder's mission statement for their family is: *We exist to love and honor Jesus Christ by living for His kingdom and letting our light shine so that others will be fully devoted to Him.*

Jason and Daniela Richardson came up with this: *To live unselfishly with grace and prayerful concern, to work as servants, and to love each person to the glory of Jesus Christ.*

Hector Ramirez is a single dad who drives home the message of the Golden Rule: *Do to others as you would have them do to you.*

Tim and Margie Hester have twelve children. No, that's not a misprint. You read it right. Twelve. One dozen. More than you can count on two hands. Besides helping the attendance numbers at the church where I preach, Tim and Margie are rearing their kids with high expectations . . . and succeeding. Here's the Hester family's mission: *Raise children who will change the world for Christ.*

Jeff and Tammy Holbrook came up with theirs when their children were very young, and they've stayed with it through the years: *To love God and one another by letting our light shine for Jesus.*

If you asked the Stone family, my kids and Beth would tell you that our mission statement is: *Go to heaven when we die and take as many people with us as we can.*

Maybe that sounds pretty general, but when you put it into practice, it makes a very specific and significant difference in the daily choices we make.

Recently, our family went out to dinner with another couple. Beth's friend later told her, "When we go out to eat at a restaurant, we go to eat. But you all go with a totally different agenda. It's like you're building relationships with the waiters and managers there."

She was exactly right. We choose where to eat based on who we need to check on or follow up with, or where we think we can plant some seed. We've nurtured relationships with staff, attended birthday parties for their children, offered help when they've faced hardships. For nearly three years, on a monthly basis, we've invested in those employees. From that particular restaurant thus far, five of them have visited our church. God has blessed us as we've tried to live out our mission.

And that's what a mission statement is designed to do— to provide a foundation for the daily choices you make and the way you live.

Evaluating How Your Family Is Doing

Every now and then you need to make certain that you are still on the right path and moving closer to your destination. Take time at a family dinner—maybe the first of each month—to evaluate how well you are accomplishing your mission. Celebrate some victories and determine some ways to improve.

For years now, the Turners have made Sunday night a family night and meeting time. They call themselves "The Turner Team," and talking about the family's mission has become common language for their young children. Sunday nights are a check-in time to see how they are doing with their mission: *To love God and love people.* The review of the week keeps their purpose before them.

They've developed six questions to discuss at their family meetings each Sunday night:

- How did we treat one another?
- Did we show God's love?
- Did we spend time with God?
- What can we work on?
- Did we make someone's day better?
- How can we pray for one another?

Our family's evaluations are less structured and less frequent than the Turners', in part because our kids at home are older than theirs. But we are quite intentional about regularly sharing with one another the relationships we're building with others, and any spiritual progress lost or made with people outside our home. Establishing the mission is important; regular checkups keep it central to the family.

Personalizing the Mission

Once you've got your mission statement, how can you avoid drifting away from your purpose? Personalize it. Connect it to daily decisions and choices, to how you live as individuals and as a family.

You may want to frame your family mission statement and place it in a prominent location, so that it becomes a frequent reminder of the goals you've set as a family. During dinner conversations, talk about how the members of your family show signs of living out the purpose. On your way to a school event or social function, remind your children of how they could put their purpose into practice. Celebrate those moments when you notice someone in your family carrying out the mission.

Part of your role as a parent is to help your children discover and recognize their own giftedness. Your family's

Establishing the mission is important; regular checkups keep it central to the family.

purpose may be the same across the board, but for each member it will play out differently.

Tell your four-year-old, "I think God was pleased when you shared your favorite toy with Colton. I think He said, 'Look, Spencer is letting his light shine!'" Say to your seven-year-old, "Whenever we're at the park, you are such a big help to Mommy in getting your younger brothers safely to the car. What a leader you are!"

One of our daughters has an amazing recall of scripture. Countless times I've heard my wife say to her, "You're a future Beth Moore." My wife is planting seeds and reinforcing purpose. I tell my teenage son, "You are so good with people. God will use that gift in you for the rest of your life."

The challenge—and fun—is finding your children's natural bent and steering them toward the family's mission. As you tailor the mission to each individual child, you can affirm them and let them know that God created them in a unique way to accomplish what others cannot.

You have more influence than you realize. Aiming your children toward a godly purpose when they are young can help direct them toward using their gifts for God in adulthood. As Max Lucado points out, "Tomorrow's Spurgeon might be mowing your lawn. And the hero who inspires him might be nearer than you think. He might be in your mirror."[2]

The Jesus Mission

When Jesus came to earth, He had a mission: "For the Son of Man came to seek and to save the lost" (Luke 19:10 NIV 2011). But it went even deeper than that. His mission was to love, and His method was making disciples—to create followers who would walk as He walked.

If His followers couldn't convey that message, what would happen to the "good news" after He ascended to heaven? Jesus intentionally spent time teaching the disciples the priorities of life. Through parables and teaching and demonstration, He trained them how to reach others. And then He began to turn things over to them. He trusted them to share the most important message of all time.

In Luke 9, toward the end of His ministry, Jesus sends His twelve disciples out to spread His message and heal the sick. They return a little defeated. They could say what He said, but they couldn't yet do what He did (Luke 9:40). Then in Luke 10, He sends them out again—seventy-two of them this time—with the purpose of spreading His message and performing miracles.

This time the whole group returns, and they are *pumped*. They've seen people respond to the message, and they've felt the power of God at work. And Luke described how Jesus felt at that moment: "full of joy through the Holy Spirit" (Luke 10:21). This is the only time the Bible gives us such an exuberant description of Jesus.

Why was Jesus so excited? Joy comes when you accomplish your mission. Jesus' joy was the result of seeing the ones He'd taught, trained, and trusted go out on this test mission and return victorious, having passed with flying colors. Not only did they do what Jesus did, but they also showed others how to do the same. His followers were filled with joy. Jesus was filled with joy. Everyone was happy.

The litmus test isn't whether the disciples can spread the message, but whether or not the *next* generation of disciples (the ones *they've* trained) can pass it on to others.

They can. They did. No wonder Jesus smiled.

Finding Joy Through Purpose

We met Jody at a golf course two thousand miles from where we live. We were on vacation, and one day Sam and I asked her how we could pray for her. She said, "You can pray for me to *find God.*"

"Are you looking for Him?" I asked

And she candidly replied, "No, I'm not."

"That will be tough," I said, "if you're not looking for Him. But our family will sure pray that."

You may be thinking, *She's not looking for God, and you may never see her again, so why waste your time praying?*

Here's why: I know something that Jody does not *yet* know.

I pray to a God who specializes in doing the impossible.

I read from a Book that says, "Nothing is impossible with God."

I worship at a church where every row has people who "found" God when they weren't really looking for Him.

And so our family regularly prays for Jody to *find God.* For Him to place people in her life who can help bring her to Him. Last week she sent me a text that shows she is taking a significant step in the right direction.

I forwarded Jody's text to my daughter Sadie. Now, Sadie's never met Jody, but she immediately called me up, elated and emotional over the progress Jody was making. Never mind that Sadie doesn't know Jody; that's irrelevant. She's a *Stone*, and she embraces our mission. Sadie's been praying so that someday, when we go to heaven, we can take Jody with us. Our kids grew up with that compass, and now it's a part of them.

Joy comes when you accomplish your mission. Purpose follows passion. Building a relationship with someone mirrors our mission.

This is the secret behind why some families appear more joyful than others. The parents have painstakingly taught and trained their children, trusting them as they proved themselves faithful. When those children grow up and have children of their own, the chain will be unbroken. The links will hold strong.

You'll see it in your house, too, with your toddler or your teen. When they accomplish the family's mission, they'll be thrilled and will announce it to you and others.

The earlier you establish your mission, the easier it becomes to define who your family is and determine the choices you make. In time you and your children will learn to run all of life's experiences through the filter of that family mission statement.

So take the time as a family to develop yours. And remember, the more detailed you can be, the more readily you will see whether or not you're achieving your goal. The more specific your family's purpose is, the deeper the joy when that purpose is fulfilled.

Find your passion as a family. Passion leads to purpose. Purpose grows into mission. Mission results in joy.

Life is full of decisions—choices to make, questions to answer, forks in the road.

So, which way from here?

That's entirely up to you.

3

Unbreakable

David woke with his heart pounding, listening in the darkness. Downstairs he could hear voices—his mom and dad—and they were arguing. He slipped from under the covers and leaned into the hall. As the voices grew louder, the tension in David's gut escalated. He shook his older brother awake, and they both eavesdropped until they could stand it no longer.

With his brother on his heels, David raced down the stairs and wedged himself between his parents. "Don't get a divorce!" he cried. "Please, don't get a divorce!"

Both the mom and dad looked bewildered—then embarrassed. "We're not mad at each other," his dad gently explained.

"We had a disagreement," his mom chimed in. "We're frustrated, and we're trying to talk it out."

The dad took both boys in his arms. "Boys, look at me," he said. "Your mother and I dearly love each other. We will never get a divorce. Never. Do you understand me?"

David and his brother nodded in agreement—and relief.

"Now, what brought this on?"

Gradually the truth came out. At school that week, one of David's friends had confided that his parents were getting divorced. David brought that anxiety home, and when he overheard his own parents arguing, he assumed the worst.

The two must have gotten in a pretty good discussion. Those happen when you are married . . . and have a pulse. But when your children are convinced you will talk, work, and pray your way through, they can live in confidence and security. What began as an unsettling evening gradually became a time of comfort and reassurance.

By the time the conversation was over, David came away with an important conviction: Mom and Dad might not always agree, but they would always work things out. Divorce was not an option.

This family was unbreakable.

Till Death Do Us Part

For a family to experience joy, there needs to be a firm foundation of security. Nobody can enjoy life to the fullest if everyone is walking on eggshells, wondering what's going to happen next, afraid that, with one wrong move, everything could fall apart. True joy in a family is founded on security. Your children need to know that *this* is their family and, Lord willing, it won't be changing.

But how do you build that kind of security in the home?

Like every other good gift of a godly family, security starts with the parents. Divorce may be a fact of life in our society, but it doesn't need to be an inevitability. Take that option off the table in your marriage. Your child needs to see you communicating and working out differences in the marriage relationship. Remind yourself that, while you have many options for conflict resolution, you don't have a back door. You don't escape when the going gets tough.

Children need to see their parents interacting, enjoying each other's conversation and company. They need a model of faithfulness and healthy negotiation of differences. And you need it too. It's not just "for the kids" that you work on your marriage; it's so that you can experience the fullness of joy that comes after you've done the difficult work of resolving conflicts.

Ephesians 4:26 reminds us, "Do not let the sun go down while you are still angry." Beth and I have tried to live by that verse. When something's wrong, we talk it out, and we don't go to bed until it's settled.

The principle has worked quite well for us.

Although there was that one time we stayed up for two weeks . . .

But it's a good rule to live by. Daily maintenance keeps you from having to do major renovations. Own your mistakes. Ask forgiveness and honestly share your feelings and fears with each other. Be real. Let your kids know that your marriage is important enough to invest in for the long haul.

When I was in high school, both of my best friends came from broken homes. Unlike me, they had incredible freedom and few restrictions. But when given the choice of where to hang out, invariably they would choose my house. At first it didn't make sense to me. Their homes were nicer. Besides, why would they want to place themselves under the restrictions of limited television viewing, clean language, and a curfew?

Soon I realized two things were present in our home and absent in theirs: joy and affection.

My friends got a kick out of seeing my parents hugging and holding each other. My initial reaction was just the opposite. I was mortified. I'd say to my parents, "Get a room," and I would quickly exit. My buddies, however, would smile, laugh, and talk with them. All the while my parents would not break their embrace.

When was the last time one of your kids walked into the kitchen and caught you and your spouse kissing? Sure, they will be grossed out and feel like they have the weirdest parents alive, but they will sleep better. They won't

True joy in a family is founded on security.

be afraid when awakened in the night by their parents' voices downstairs.

Flying Solo

You may say, "Well, that leaves me out; I'm divorced" or "My spouse is pulling away from me." That makes it more of a challenge, certainly, but not impossible. If you're divorced or estranged, you may have to work harder to get along with your ex, but it's work worth doing. Parental conflict chips away at a child's security.

Please know that if you are a single parent, my heart goes out to you. I'm sure it's not easy. God will give you better direction than I can. He is always with you. He understands.

But let me assure you that even though you are a single parent, your home can still become a secure haven. You are not alone in this parenting venture. If the Lord is at the center of your life, then you have a Teammate beside you who enables you to do more than two could ever do without Christ. He can fill in the gaps caused from divorce, the death of a spouse, or a mate who is still physically present but on a different spiritual wavelength.

And there are practical ways you can work to give your children that sense of family security:

- Pray with your children for the *other* parent, and be genuinely thankful for him or her. Help your children—with God's help—to do thoughtful things and express acceptance and forgiveness.
- Do your best to work through conflicts without involving the children. Ask the Lord to strengthen your bonds with Him and your spouse or ex. Invite His involvement.
- Seek out an older Christian couple who can come alongside and invest in the life of your kids. Maybe they don't have grandchildren in town, but they have a whole lot of love and encouragement to share. Both of you will be blessed by the relationship.

In order to foster security in a single-parent home, you may need to put dating on the back burner for a while. Divided loyalties can unintentionally erode a child's sense of security. How long? It depends. It might be two years. It might be ten years. But however long it is, that intentional act can communicate to your children that they are important and valuable to you.

When my friend Jackie was single, there was a period of time where she consistently turned down every man who asked her out. She longed for a fresh start and a loving relationship, but she felt that her three children desperately needed Mom's attention more than she needed male attention.

When the time is right for you to start dating again, keep your standards high. Remember that you are now modeling in real time how you want your children to approach dating. Little eyes are watching.

Finally, remember the promise found in Hebrews 13:5. Paste it on the bathroom mirror. Make that verse your screensaver: "Never will I leave you; never will I forsake you."

Your ex may have left you, but God never will. Whether your monthly child support checks are wishful thinking or direct deposited, the Lord will meet your needs. And although you may feel judged by a church, or abandoned by family members, or stressed from trying to be two parents instead of one—rest assured that the Lord will *never* forsake you.

He can't. It's a divine impossibility for Him—He loves you too much.

Parenting 101: Fear or Trust

Some of you didn't have a Christian upbringing with the security you now have in Christ. You have embraced faith, broken the cycle, and are raising kids in a different manner than you were raised. Good for you. That's a God-honoring way to change the growth of the family tree. But first-generation Christian parents face particular challenges.

Recently I spoke with my friend Susan St. Clair who, along with her husband, Lance, authored *Blending by the Book*. (And, no, it's not about all the great things you can do with a Cuisinart!) It's about following the Lord's way as you set about creating a blended family.

Susan says there's a tendency for first-generation Christians to parent out of fear, to "rubber-band back" to their *own* behaviors and mistakes as adolescents. They give in to worry and doubt because biblical principles weren't modeled for them. The result is, they second-guess their parenting:

- Are my kids running with the same kind of friends I had as a teen?
- Can I trust them to not get into trouble?
- Will they do what I did on prom night?

"The enemy [Satan] is the author of fear," she says. "First-generation Christian parents have learned to instill biblical values into the hearts of their children. They do all the right things when the children are very young, but then freak out when the kids hit fourteen. That has such a terrible effect."

Susan concludes: "If you plant apple seeds, it will be an *apple* tree that emerges from the soil—not an *orange* tree. Trust that what you planted will develop."[3]

This is a significant principle, not just for first-generation Christian parents, but for those of us who carry a legacy of godliness as well. The Bible says, "Perfect love drives out fear" (1 John 4:18). God doesn't parent out of fear—and neither should we. We can trust that the seeds we plant in our children's lives will come to fruition.

All children will have their areas of temptation and weakness. Don't blindly assume that they will be able to navigate through on their own. Get involved, be proactive, share with them how you've learned to overcome certain temptations. Then trust that in due time you will reap the benefits. The more authentic and intentional you have been about passing the spiritual baton, the less you should sweat the small stuff of life. Show your kids the joy of the Lord, and their security will be bolstered as they pursue it.

When to Trust and Not to Trust

When my oldest daughter was seventeen, she had been dating her future husband for about a year. She asked permission for the two of them to travel together on a day trip. She looked at Beth and me and said, "Don't you trust me?"

And without hesitation we both responded, "No, we don't . . . and we don't trust Patrick either."

That wasn't being harsh; it was being honest. Savannah was, and is, a delightful, responsible girl and a dedicated Christian. But the truth is, we wouldn't have trusted *ourselves* if we'd been placed in a similar setting, so as loving parents, we didn't want to set her up for failure. The consequences of sexual sin are much greater than being late for curfew on a Friday night or blowing off a homework assignment. As her loving parents, we realized it was too great a temptation for us to ignore.

As a godly parent you have planted good seed, and you want to trust God for the harvest. Assure your children that you trust them to make wise choices, that you believe in them. But that trust doesn't mean that you intentionally place them in settings where they will be intensely tempted. Security grows as your children prove themselves worthy of more freedom.

Let me add one additional warning. Don't fall into the trap of lowering your expectations—"Kids have to sow their wild oats," or "All teens rebel at some point—it's part of growing up," or "Courtney just turned sixteen; I had better get her on the pill—*just to be safe.*"

Take a step back and recognize that this is the world's deceptive thinking. You will get what you expect.

Harry Emerson Fosdick wrote, "One thing is better than bringing the prodigal son back from the far country, and that is keeping him from going there in the first place."[4]

Don't give your teens permission to dramatically alter their lives (and yours) through your low expectations. Instead, set the bar high, and guide them through loving boundaries. Down deep children want parameters. They need security. Boundaries don't reduce joy; they reveal it and unleash it.

Freedom to Fail

Setting boundaries doesn't require a helicopter. Hovering over your children doesn't teach them responsibility; it suffocates them. Typically it leads to rebellion because they can't wait for the day when they are free from the bondage of your watchful eye. The solution is to gradually give them more and more privileges as they prove themselves responsible. Eventually that freedom fosters a secure feeling. You aren't expecting perfection, just respect, communication, and a desire to obey.

I have a friend who used to construct buildings in California. Because of the frequency of earthquakes there, tall buildings are actually built on rollers, so that there is some flexibility to the structure when a tremor occurs. While the foundation is solid, it also has some margin for movement. In the moment of trauma, the building will sway instead of breaking.

So when you feel the earth move under your feet because of your son or daughter's unwise actions, remain confident in your planning and preparation. Expect tremors. Quakes will rumble and buildings will sway, but if you've laid the right foundation, they need not fall. How you handle the tremors caused by your children will reveal how secure the home is.

Will you be disappointed? Sure.

Frustrated? Of course.

Embarrassed by their actions? Occasionally.

But remember, your worth and identity are found in being a child of God, not a perfect parent with perfect children. They've got free will too. If you work through those smaller challenges and mistakes, you'll help pave the way for them to make wiser choices in the future.

Parenting is a process of preparing your children for the next step in their development. It's a gradual releasing of them from childhood. If timed correctly, the transition into adulthood can occur quite naturally. Then when they call, Skype, or return to spend time with you, it's on their terms. It's their choice. The communication and interaction are out of desire, not obligation. Your fulfillment as a parent goes to a whole new level because of the healthy way you raised them.

Clinging to the Rock

Despite the technological advances of the twenty-first century, we live in an age of fear—of deadbolts and LoJacks, spycams and home security systems. But the Bible clearly tells us what the source of our safety and security is: "My soul finds rest in God alone; my salvation comes from him. He alone is my rock and my salvation; he is my fortress, I will never be shaken" (Psalm 62:1–2).

Years ago when my daughter Savannah was only four, our family was at a swimming pool. At one point, everyone else had left but us. I was down in the deep end holding onto the diving board, just enjoying the water. Savannah had put on her big orange floaties—you know, those inflatable cuffs that fit on your child's upper arms. Those dudes could keep an elephant from sinking.

Well, Savannah came bobbing her way into the shallow end. She kind of splashed around for a few minutes, while I was way down there in the deep end. Then she said, "Daddy, I'm scared! I want to come to where you are."

I replied, "Well, honey, it's a lot deeper down here."

And without hesitation she said, "I don't care. I want to be where *you* are."

I said, "Great! Come on over."

So she started dogpaddling her way across that water with a worried expression on her face—three feet deep, six feet, nine feet, twelve feet deep. When she got to me, she grabbed onto my neck. Immediately her look of panic gave way to relief. And she smiled.

You know why? Next to her father she felt secure. It made very little difference how deep or how dangerous the water was as long as she was holding onto someone more powerful whom she trusted.

Conflict, when approached with commitment and resolved with compassion, actually strengthens the foundation of the marriage and the family.

I don't know what type of waters your family has faced or will face—but I do know this. There will be times when your kids will need to cling to you. They'll look to you to be the rock and the fortress. And you can be that for them, just as God is for you.

Your love, time, and wisdom can buoy them when the waters of this world become choppy and frightening.

Sure, there will be the occasional argument or "discussion"; it may even wake up the kids. But conflict, when approached with commitment and resolved with compassion, actually strengthens the foundation of the marriage and the family.

And what about those arguing parents I spoke of earlier? They kept their promise. They kept their family unbreakable. In fact, they've been married for fifty-four years and counting.

I ought to know. I call them Mom and Dad.

4

Laugh Like You Mean It

At the tender age of sixteen, Matt landed his first job as a delivery boy for a florist. Things were going pretty well until one day he had two deliveries to make on the same run. One of the arrangements was to go to a church that was having a big dedication service for their new sanctuary. The other, to a funeral home.

A few hours later the florist got a phone call from an irate preacher. "We have a big problem," the pastor said. "Our dedication service starts in thirty minutes, and up in the front of our new sanctuary is this huge basket of flowers that says, 'Rest in Peace.'"

"You think you've got problems?" the florist said. "Somewhere in this town next to a casket, there's an arrangement that says, 'Good Luck in Your New Location!'"

A study conducted by the University of Maryland shows that laughter is good for the heart. Laughter releases chemicals into the bloodstream that relax the blood vessels. It reduces stress, blood pressure, and heart rate and can improve your immune system.[5] The Bible said it, and medical science confirms it: "A cheerful heart is good medicine, but a crushed spirit dries up the bones" (Proverbs 17:22). No wonder a sense of humor is consistently one of the top characteristics desired in friendships, among coworkers, and in a spouse.

Take a Lesson from Jesus

In case you are *humorically* challenged, a brief tutorial on the subject might help. Longtime Christian comedian and speaking coach Ken Davis understands the role of humor in speaking. Years ago he shared with me that in order for something to be funny, it must always have one of three elements: exaggeration, truth, or surprise.

My kids were very young when I taught them the Big Three. They learned those faster than their social security number. And for years the premise has been validated—anything we laugh about falls into one of those three categories.

Jesus had a great sense of humor. He captivated crowds for hours. Children flocked to Him. He excelled at building relationships with people of all backgrounds. Why? Because love and laughter can break down the strongest of defenses.

Love and laughter can break down the strongest of defenses.

People often ask me if Jesus ever used humor when He taught. Fact is, He actually used all of the Big Three in His talks. He primarily used *exaggeration*, because in first-century Jewish culture, humor was based on hyperbole. Jesus was a master at the technique; the bigger the exaggeration, the funnier the joke. So when Jesus said, "Why do you look at the speck of sawdust in your brother's eye and fail to notice the plank in your own?" (Matthew 7:5 PHILLIPS), people in the crowd weren't reverently murmuring, "Amen." They were cracking up because of the gross exaggeration.

Jesus spoke with vivid, humorous word pictures to drive home His message: "It is easier for a camel to go through the eye of a needle than for a rich man to enter the kingdom of God" (Matthew 19:24). The contrast would have elicited laughter from His listeners, and the laughter would provide an opening for the truth. Jesus knew that humor was a disarming equalizer—perhaps that's why He used it throughout His ministry. Maybe that's why He was so approachable.

In Matthew 23, in His denunciation of the Pharisees, He used the element of *surprise*. Here were the respected religious leaders of the day, and Jesus compared them with whitewashed tombs that look good on the outside, yet are filled with dead men's bones. While the crowd might not have laughed in front of the Pharisees, they would have gone home, retold the story, and laughed about how the Teacher's unexpected words caught everyone off guard.

Then Jesus rounded out the trifecta by simply stating the *truth*. When behaviors are already ridiculous, sometimes the truth can be downright side-splitting. All Jesus had to do was point out the legalism of the Pharisees' tithing practices—all the way down to giving 10 percent of each stalk from their gardens!

Did Jesus have a sense of humor? You bet He did. Hebrews 1:9 even points out that God the Father anointed Jesus with "the oil of gladness beyond [His] companions" (ESV). He must have been joyful—even absolutely hilarious.

Goofing Around

Being a preacher I do a lot of weddings and funerals, and sometimes people ask me which I prefer. The easy answer is "Funerals, because there's one fewer person to complain if things go wrong."

Since my pet peeve is "generic funerals," I always ask the immediate family—usually the adult children of the dearly departed—to share their favorite memories going back to childhood. Once someone begins sharing funny memories, the floodgates open.

"Every July 4 we'd go camping at the river, and Mom would act like she didn't know how to cook on a grill—so the other ladies would do it for her!"

"My Uncle Phil had memorized entire scenes from *The Princess Bride.*

"Dad bought a deep fryer, and he would deep fry anything. He would freeze a Snickers bar and then deep fry it!"

The more they share, the more they laugh. There will still be tears, but there's also joy from the memories made and the traditions kept.

This is a common thread for families who enjoy spending time together. The technical term is . . . goofiness. Even the most staid individuals, the ones who aren't exactly known for being hilarious or entertaining, sometimes let their hair down around family members.

Laughter helps a house become a home.

Spontaneity

The great preacher Vance Havner, known for his incisive one-liners, said, "A rut is nothing but a grave with both ends kicked out."[6] If you want to get your family laughing, you've got to get out of that rut. Be spontaneous. Change things up.

When I was very young, our family would take off in the car for our summer vacation in the family station wagon. After a while Dad would get a worried look on his face. "Oh no!" he'd say. "There's something wrong with the steering wheel of the car. I can't control where it's going."

After the first few times this happened, we would start giggling, because we were familiar with the script, and we loved the ending. But Dad would stay in character; he'd turn down some street, shouting, "What's happening? The car is out of control!" In a matter of seconds he would pull the car into some remote Dairy Queen restaurant that he'd masterfully located.

He'd turn to Mom. "Honey, I know we don't have money to be buying ice cream, but this car has a mind of its own!" We'd squeal and cheer and then go indulge in some decadent desserts.

If you have young kids, some of your spontaneous activities will not require much advance planning. Take advantage of that luxury now! Come bedtime, say, "Get your PJs on and meet me at the car. We're going to the drive-through at Krispy Kreme doughnuts." Or, on the spur of the moment, surprise the kids with an overnight campout. Pitch a tent in the yard and make s'mores on the grill.

Unfortunately, the older the child gets, the more reluctant we parents are to risk doing something spontaneous. We fear having our crazy whims backfire, and so we're hesitant to step out in faith. We struggle to keep up with what our kids like this week—or maybe even this afternoon! But don't let it keep you from taking some risks and raising the joy quotient for your family. And remember that even when you get it right, your teens may never let on that they're really having fun.

Here's a radical concept: In order for your family to have fun together, they must spend time together. So get out of your comfort zone and breathe life, joy, and camaraderie into your family.

I call it "planned spontaneity." On numerous occasions I've surprised one of my kids by taking them with me on a one- or two-day business trip. (If you drive, it doesn't cost any more money except for food.) That extended time together, just the two of us, always deepened the family ties. At first they might not have been excited, but once they got out of town, everything changed.

Avoid the ruts and take some risks. The money you'll spend on a Dairy Queen Blizzard is a drop in the bucket compared to paying for braces or college tuition. Your kids will never forget the car that had a mind of its own or the parent who cared enough to make a road trip fun.

Create Memories That Last

hat are the memories that mean most to the Stone family?

- Game nights at our home with neighbors or new friends
- Having the employees of our favorite restaurant over

to our home for a party in their honor
- Friday night "family night" when the kids were young
- The annual Christmas gift delivery and caroling around town wearing goofy elf hats (If one of us is going to look stupid, we all are. There's safety in numbers!)
- Stopping at O'Charley's Restaurant on our family's drive back from picking up one of the kids from summer camp (The rest of us would eat while the camper recapped the entire week—in detail.)
- Our annual hide-and-seek game at church on the evening of Christmas Day (My master key may be the greatest perk of my job!)
- The entire family camping out on the floor of my office to stay up and watch the opening afternoon and evening of March Madness (You're a good sport, Beth!)

Beth and I have always tried to have a purpose behind our activities. We've planned conversations and competitions, vacations with a purpose, even the trivia test I'd unveil on the final day of vacation (with a whopping $10 prize to the winner). We knew that every experience can be both a teaching opportunity and a bonding time for your family.

Whether it's an annual activity or a spur-of-the-moment surprise, be intentional about it. Use it as a chance to connect with your family and help them connect with God. When the kids were toddlers, we'd sit on a blanket imagining we were on a raft surrounded by water—and the living room became a world of adventure. That's a great adventure for preschoolers, but—news flash—it ain't gonna fly with your teenage son.

One of our main staples for years has been inviting people to come over for a game night. Some games are brainteasers, and others are just downright simple so the intellectual giants tend to struggle. On those nights we laugh hard, and usually one of the guests will burn our family with a mind game.

One night we had the Duggar family to our home for dinner. You may have seen their television program on the TLC network, *19 Kids and Counting*. The house was packed with people and, more importantly, with laughter. It didn't take long for us to see that the Duggars have a blast together as a family. They are quite intentional about serving and laughing together. After two hours of *our* games, they suckered me into a game they called "I Saw a Bear"—which might have alternately been called "I Embarrassed Dave."

To add to my humiliation, Jim Bob Duggar videotaped it on his phone and then showed it to my congregation in a church service. (That is *so* unspiritual, to make fun of a pastor! Ha-ha.)

Despite my humiliation—or perhaps because of it—everyone had a wonderful time. It's a memory we'll cherish for years.

Laughter and joy shouldn't be guests in your house; they should be permanent residents in your everyday life.

Believe it or not, you *can* have fun without a TV, computer, iPad, or other electronic device. You can teach your children how to communicate with adults and how to be comfortable in their own skin.

You can establish family bonds and create lasting memories. And you can make those traditions unique to your family, so that your kids will carry on the tradition as they become adults.

Laughter and joy shouldn't be guests in your house; they should be permanent residents in your everyday life.

The Limits of Laughter

It was the midseventies: I was fifteen and Jeff was seventeen. The church we were attending was between preachers, so each Sunday our dad would close out the worship service by reading the first-time visitor cards and asking the individuals to stand. This became the setting for a wonderful, wicked idea.

Jeff and I knew that our father understood absolutely nothing about rock-and-roll music. So each week we filled out one bogus visitor card with a false name. Since we are true connoisseurs of practical jokes, our hope was to milk this for as long as we could.

The first week at the end of the service, Dad began to read the names, and the church acknowledged the visitors.

When he came to our card, he said, "Okay, would Pete Frampton please stand?"

No one stood up, of course. Jeff and I (along with all of our high school buddies) fought back the laughter. Dad, oblivious to what was going on, said, "Oh, I guess he had to leave early."

The next week we came back with another strong entry. That Sunday, as Dad recognized visitors, he read the name of Alice Cooper. The icing on the cake was when he said, "Is *she* here?" All of us teens were nearly on the floor of the sanctuary attempting to stifle our laughter.

But the third week we went too far. The scene replayed itself, but this time as Dad was recognizing the guests, he came to our card and stared at it a little too long. His face turned red. He glared in our direction and moved on to the next card.

Uh-oh.

I turned to Jeff and whispered, "Evidently he's heard of Ozzy Osbourne."

And the consequences? I'd rather not go into it, if you don't mind. Let's just say that my brother and I repented. We learned the hard way what it means to go and sin no more.

Humor is a lot like gasoline: The right amount used at the right time and for the right purpose can be a great blessing and resource. But if used improperly or as a weapon, it can start a fire that's tough to extinguish.

Laughing *with* someone is exhilarating; laughing *at* someone is disrespectful. As a parent you must be aware that criticism and ridicule tears the fabric of the family. If you allow your children to mock or disrespect their siblings or your authority as the parent, then you will diminish the joy and weaken the family bond.

Regardless of what they may let on, kids' egos are fragile during adolescence. Your children will progress through seasons of awkwardness and stages of hypersensitivity. At times a child's self-confidence will be shaky at best. But when they see you laughing about your own idiosyncrasies, then it becomes easier for them to do the same concerning their own flaws and quirks.

Like me, many of you have been blessed (or cursed) with the gift of sarcasm. If you have this gift, you are no doubt well aware of it, because your spouse has pointed it out to you more than once. Admittedly, sarcasm does not appear in any of the biblical passages that list spiritual gifts, but with all the new translations and paraphrases, it's only a matter of time until it shows up . . .

Solomon said, "Like a madman shooting firebrands or deadly arrows is a man who deceives his neighbor and says, 'I was only joking!'" (Proverbs 26:18). Teach your family that laughter, which leads to joy, will refresh and not wound.

Laughter Starts Now

At this point, some of you will commence with the excuses:

"Dave, I'm an introvert."

"Humor doesn't come naturally for me."

"Some of the things you've mentioned wouldn't work with our family."

Well, I understand that we're all wired differently. You don't have to do everything I've mentioned, but you can do *something*. You can get out of your comfort zone and attempt to take a baby step and try one of the ideas in this chapter.

My good friend Rick Atchley asks this question: "Anyone else notice the time warp of parenting? The days are so long, but the years are so short."[7]

Now is the time to get serious about having some fun. Let your hair down. Be goofy. Laugh like you mean it.

Time's a-wastin'. Don't put it off. Set down the remote and slowly back away from the couch. Take a break from paying the bills. Put this book aside—for a little while anyway—and step into your child's life.

Your tasks and responsibilities will still be waiting for you when you return. Your effort at family time will not be forgotten by your kids. It will pave the way for more smiles, giggles, and laughter.

If he's four, get out a blanket and set sail on the living room floor. If she's eight, go find a box of old clothes and play dress-up. If he's thirteen, ask him to teach you how to play his favorite video game.

And if your kids are breathing . . . go get ice cream together.

5

The Hour of Power

Time for a pop quiz. You don't need paper or a #2 pencil, and it's only one question. . . .

What is the *one thing* you can do as a parent that accomplishes all of the following:

- Gives your child a 40 percent greater chance of getting As and Bs in school[8]
- Makes your child three times less likely to try marijuana, two times less likely to smoke cigarettes, and one time less likely to drink alcohol
- Helps teenagers know that their parents are proud of them
- Helps teenagers to realize that they can confide in their parents about a serious problem[9]
- Helps reduce your child's chance of obesity by 40 percent[10]

What is that one thing?

I'll tell you what it's *not*: It's not praying with them. It's not going to church, having a mission statement, or wearing a name badge with "Family" listed as your passion. Those things are important, but the statistical benefits listed above are all tied to one specific activity:

Eating!

That's right—shared meals are essential for a healthy family. Gathering around the dinner table isn't just something we see in reruns of black-and-white TV shows. What takes place while your family is seated around that table will bear more fruit than you could possibly imagine.

The blessings of the dinner table are both obvious and numerous. Around the table we can teach manners, model principles, discuss topics, and honor God.

Dr. Catherine Snow, professor of education at Harvard Graduate School of Education, followed sixty-five families over an eight-year period. She found that there was something of more value to child development than playtime, school, or story time.

The big winner was family dinner.[11]

Several separate studies confirm the profound effects of dinnertime together. Eating regular meals together gives parents and kids time to talk and relate to one another without distractions. Kids who sit down at the table with their families do better in school and in life, are more stable, and are less apt to get into trouble. The leading common

The dinner table provides a setting for you to show your dependence on God.

denominator among high achievers is not wealth, appearance, or intelligence; it's the simple fact of eating dinner together as a family.

In other words, dinnertime is more than just a meal.

Soup and Salad: Getting Started

Saying Grace

O kay, who would like to say grace?"

When I was growing up, our family never called our prayer time around the table "grace," but yours may have. I like it. The word itself sounds like a blessing.

When you pause to pray, you are establishing a healthy habit and expressing thanks both to the One who provided the food and to those who prepared it. The dinner table provides a setting for you to show your dependence on God. The Bible says, "Every good and perfect gift is from above" (James 1:17).

If your children don't agree that food is a good gift, perhaps it's time for the family to *fast* from a meal. Nothing teaches appreciation quicker than going without something you take for granted.

And while you're thanking God for your blessings, remember that not everyone has a good meal on the table—or even a table to put it on. You don't have to go to a developing nation to find people who are hungry. All you have to do is drive around your own town. It's important to remind your family of the plight of others who are less fortunate, and to remember that part of our calling as followers of Jesus is to care for those who are hungry and hurting.

Also, take turns praying at dinner. Teach your young children that the meal begins with gratitude. It can be something as simple as going around the table and saying one thing you're thankful for that day. It can be holding hands for a moment of quiet meditation, with each silently talking to God, or singing a familiar chorus that expresses your thankfulness.

Don't fixate on how flowery or big the words. Simply say grace—and as you pray, thank God for His.

The Place to Be

Until your family becomes accustomed to the expectations of family mealtime, you may have to establish some guidelines. For instance, don't let your kids rush through the mealtime experience just to get to something else they want to do. You might say, "On the nights we all get to eat together, we won't leave the table for at least thirty or forty-five minutes."

The time you spend at the table, of course, will vary based on the ages of your children. But prepare yourself for the inevitable question from your impatient fourteen-year-old, "May I be excused?"

Sometimes the answer is "No, because you haven't expressed any interest in anyone else. So we'll stay here until you've given us the attention you're about to give that video game or your best friend." Be patient and stick to your principles, and the dinner table can become a place of joy and security.

Once when Sam was six, he was struggling with some self-control issues at the dinner table. We sent him upstairs for a time-out. The toughest part of the punishment, as it turned out, was the fact that he was still able to hear everyone else laughing and talking downstairs. Sam wanted to be at that table where the fun was. He was missing out. Through our intentionality, we had created an environment that caused a child to *want* to be there.

Three Words

Last night I sent a text to my daughters and asked my son this question: In your opinion, what three words describe our dinnertimes together? A few minutes later each one had weighed in—one from Texas, one from college in Tennessee, and one at home.

- Savannah: interactive, humorous, and relational
- Sadie: laughter, relaxing, and joy-filled
- Sam: family, fellowship, and fun

So, how do you create that?

Be patient and stick to your principles, and the dinner table can become a place of joy and security.

Meat and Potatoes: The Basics

Making the Time Productive

If you want to see fruit from your family gatherings, you'll need to put some effort and thought into dinnertime—and I'm not referring to the menu. It doesn't really matter whether you cook or bring it in. There are more important things that deserve your attention.

As a child I was always intrigued by the personal attention my parents gave each other and us kids. At night when we would be eating dinner together, my dad would pull a three-by-five card out of his pocket. On it would be four or five words he had scribbled down during his day in order to simply jog his memory. Throughout the meal, Dad would share with us events of the day or some news he'd received. He'd say, "The Meyers had a baby girl, and she's doing great" or "I read today that a new Disney movie is coming out this weekend."

That small card filled with chicken scratches let us know that, during different moments of the day, we were on his mind. He thought about us and wanted to share something specifically with us. Those brief conversations made huge deposits in the family "security" account.

You may be thinking, "This isn't practical for my three- year-old" or "My two teenagers would feel like this is childish."

Well, there's not a *one size fits all* when it comes to family dinnertimes. But try *something*. Put some thought into creating your own "index card" moments.

Here are some ideas you might tailor for your family:

The Talking Bowl. Create a "talking bowl"—a small bowl that sits in the center of your dinner table where everyone in the family puts in a question. Every time you gather for dinner, pull out one of the questions and discuss it. The questions can be serious, like "What do you think heaven is like?" or "What's your greatest hope for the future?" Or they can be silly, such as "What would it feel like to be a cloud?" or "What's the family dog dreaming about while she sleeps?" There are no right or wrong answers. Everyone has a voice. And along the way, you may learn a thing or two about the people you *think* you know.

High/Low. Go around the table and have each person tell about the lowest moment in the day. The next time around, share the highest point of the day. In this simple way, you and your family crack open the door to your hearts and allow your loved ones a peek inside and see what brings joy or pain. It is a great opportunity to let prayer requests emerge from the lows that are shared—and then to speak of how God is beside you in the mountains and valleys of life. It also teaches your kids to take an interest in their siblings and parents.

Celebrate Good Times. Once a month when I was a kid, my mom would choose to honor someone in the family who had achieved something of significance. If my brother got his driver's license, for example, or Dad received a promotion . . . or I got a C on a test . . . we'd celebrate!

If you were the fortunate recipient, dinner would consist of your favorite main course and dessert (home-cooked or carryout). Mom would have toilet paper streaming down from the dining room light to each corner of the table. She made mealtimes a time of fun and interaction. Besides, toilet paper is cheaper than streamers!

The keys to creating an atmosphere of anticipation around mealtime together are positivity, acceptance, and variety.

And good-tasting food helps too!

Fun at Restaurants

Another way to connect with your family is to go out to eat occasionally—and drive-through at a fast-food restaurant doesn't count.

When the kids were young, we knew which restaurants had "kids eat free" nights. It helped the budget and gave the kids familiar stomping grounds. At one hamburger place we frequented on Tuesday nights, they'd announce your order by calling out the name of someone in your party. We would take turns each month so that all the kids would get to hear their names announced over the loudspeaker. Then, as they got older, they got pretty creative in making up fake names:

"Elvis, your order is ready."

"Could Madonna please come to the counter?"

"Order for Yogi Bear. Yogi, please."

They had not just our family but the whole restaurant in stitches.

Keep it simple; make it fun. It's good training for your kids, and it doesn't have to cost a fortune for a memorable night out.

Fruits & Vegetables: What's Good For You

From "Me" to "We"

Beth did a great job of involving the kids in the dinner process, whether it was with the cooking, setting the table, or cleaning up. When the girls were very little, she would assign one of them to come up with a centerpiece—and we ended up with some pretty unusual ones! They sparked great conversations!

It's natural for children to focus on themselves. But part of maturing is learning to be aware of others and sensitive to their needs. Sitting around the table affords opportunities for your children to work on areas of obedience, communication, and selflessness.

When our children were younger, whenever we had a guest for dinner or would go to someone's home, we would prep them beforehand. They were expected to have a couple of specific questions in mind to ask the individual through the course of the meal. This encourages an outward emphasis rather than an "everything revolves around me" mentality.

Changing from "me" to "we" is a huge step in the transition from child to teen and teen to adult. Dinnertime is the perfect setting for fostering that maturing process along—for teaching your children how to carry on a conversation, how to show interest in other people, and how to share the spotlight with those around them. It also gives them a sense of belonging—the recognition that, *As part of this family, I belong to an important "we." I'm not alone, and what I do affects the people I love.*

Share the Joy

Once you get dinnertime established, encourage your children to invite a neighborhood friend to a meal. This adds to the conversation and gives you the chance to teach your kids how to ask insightful questions that focus on the guest and not themselves.

Through shared meals, you can enable your kids to reach out to their friends. You can show them how to steer conversations in a spiritual direction. Whoever was the guest for the meal was served on a decorative plate that said "You Are Special," and we would each pray sentence prayers and thank God for something we appreciated about the individual. It's a simple but effective way to plant spiritual seeds in the lives of your children's friends.

Remind one another of your values as a family and the ways you've determined God is leading you.

Priorities and Mission

Dinnertime gives you a regular time to discuss current events and hear about your family's day. You can check in on their struggles or progress at school and learn what kinds of challenges they're facing. It keeps your priorities front and center.

If you've developed your own family mission statement, dinnertime is a perfect opportunity to talk about it.

- Repeat the mission.
- Review how everyone is doing.
- Reinforce the purpose behind it.
- Reward those family members who recently modeled the mission.

This could become a regular weekly exercise. Remind one another of your values as a family and the ways you've determined God is leading you. Make connections between your mission statement and your everyday lives. Mealtime is a great chance to validate your family's direction.

Q&A

When our kids were younger, we often used dinnertime to role-play certain scenarios, to challenge and prepare our children for adversity and opposition before the situation arose. So around the dinner table, we might describe a potential setting that our thirteen-year-old might encounter. Beth might say, "Savannah, you are at a party and a couple of kids pull out some marijuana and try to get you to smoke it."

Savannah had to reply with how she would respond in that situation, while all the rest of us got into the game, playing the role of the other partyers. We would make fun of her and entice her to participate.

After she responded, the rest of the family talked about what she did right and coached her on additional things she might say.

I have to admit, all our kids got into the spirit of this exercise. They all have a quick—and warped—sense of humor (wonder where they got that?), and at times they'd switch sides and tease Beth by saying, "Sure, I'd love some marijuana. Do you have any more?"

The role-play exercise lasted until they were thirteen or fourteen and got too old for it. We always matched the scenario to what we thought would be the next set of temptations they were likely to face.

The purpose was to be proactive, to teach before the situation arose. It turned out to be an immensely profitable use of our dinnertime—and a whole lot of fun.

Protecting Dinnertime

As your children grow older, there will be more obstacles to interaction around the table. If you have a one-year-old and a four-year-old, dinner together may be most nights. If you have a middle schooler, two high schoolers, and a parent whose job requires some travel, getting two or three nights together for dinner each week may be the best you can do.

Since we just have one teen (age seventeen) still at home, we've gotten creative about mealtimes. Varsity sports and Sam's work schedule make it difficult. So now we eat breakfast together three mornings a week. We use this time to pray together. Three or four nights a week we get to have dinner together as well.

But crazy schedules aren't the only obstacles. Distractions will infiltrate your kitchen setting like crabgrass in your yard—and the majority of those interruptions will make ringing, dinging, or vibrating noises. Stress to your kids that face-to-face is more important than Facebook!

And let me challenge you to make the dinner table a technology-free zone. Our culture feeds the false premise that the earth will stop rotating if that tweet isn't read or that text isn't answered instantly. But, trust me, it can be immensely freeing for your family when you decide not to answer phones or texts during a meal.

And, yes, I'll admit it—some of us still twitch when we hear them ringing. But we've survived, and our family is closer because of it.

THE HOUR OF POWER

Dessert: Making Sweet Memories

Some years ago C. Ray Hall, a local journalist, was assigned to write a feature story on me. (It must have been a slow news week.) In an effort to get to know me, he scheduled a couple of two-hour interviews. Toward the end of our first meeting, I commented that my family was the best thing I had going for me.

"I'd love for you to meet them," I said. Then I blurted out, "Would you like to eat dinner with us?"

He surprised me by saying yes.

At the time our children were ages two, five, and eight.

I know, I know. Every female reader is now thinking, "Are you out of your mind?"

Fortunately, Beth has the gift of hospitality. I called her and got the green light.

An hour later, Mr. Hall arrived with a cherry pie, courtesy of the local grocery store. His generosity ensured that he got the "special" plate . . . and, much to his relief, didn't get asked to pray. Instead, all five of us prayed for him.

From Mr. Hall's perspective, that might have been the highlight of the night. The innocence and purity of children praying for a new friend can be profound.

He didn't seem to mind crowding around a little table. He even heeded our warning not to move his knee a certain way for fear it could cause one side of the table to collapse. The kids asked him questions, everybody laughed a lot, and we all had an enjoyable evening.

Twelve years later, my wife and I ran into him. He remembered that evening in detail. Even recalled what Beth had cooked and some of the questions our children had asked him during dinner. Evidently, making memories at mealtimes extends far beyond your immediate family.

The table really can be a place of deepening relationships, sharing encouragement, and laughing uncontrollably. If you create an appetite not just for dinner, but for dinnertime, your meal will do more than just satisfy your family's physical cravings. It will fulfill their relational needs too.

Dinnertime is about more than just food. It's an hour of real spiritual power. It's a place where you can build family ties with faith, love, and laughter. It sets the stage for praying together, developing a family mission statement, learning to confront challenges, and truly enjoying one another.

So . . . who's Hungry?

6

Cultivating Contentment

When the invitation for the birthday party came in the mail, it surprised everyone. It read:

> Instead of bringing a birthday gift, please bring a gift card for a grocery store, and we'll share it with our local food pantry.
> —Kathryn

Pretty remarkable, isn't it? Apparently the guests thought so too. They caught the spirit and brought in a total of $360 in gift cards. Kathryn and her friends gave joy to several families that Thanksgiving with their creative generosity.

But here's the truly remarkable part: Kathryn was twelve years old.

At a time in life when most adolescents are concerned solely about their own desires, about getting what they want and keeping it for themselves, this young girl used her birthday party to offer food to others rather than hoard gifts for herself.

Where did she get such an idea?

Well, the year before her older sister Sarah had said, "For my birthday party we're going to the mall to pick out an angel from the Angel Tree so we can go together to adopt a family and buy gifts for Christmas."

Two teenagers in the same family, demonstrating contentment with what they have and a generosity of spirit that leads them to share with others. It's not a fluke, an accident, or an anomaly. It's the way they've been brought up.

Want your kids to grow into Kathryns and Sarahs? Want them to mature and derive joy through giving rather than keeping? Want them to become generous, giving, and gracious people?

It starts with you.

With your values. With your priorities. With your awareness that enough is enough.

Contentment is contagious.

Unfortunately, it's also pretty rare.

The "Me" Message

It's all too easy for parents to communicate the wrong messages to their children. When we try to keep up with the Joneses rather than rejoicing over their blessings, we send the message that material possessions are more important than spiritual riches. When we act as if joy is dependent on what we have, where we live, and how we feel, we model self-centeredness for our children. When we hang on to what we have rather than sharing it with others, we shout, loud and clear, that it's all about *me*.

If you want your family to experience true joy, you have to shift the spotlight from yourselves to others.

One of the most damaging things you can do as a parent is to give your children the best of everything. Instead, teach them the value of working, saving, and giving. Show them, by your own example, the blessings that come with sharing what they have with others. Let them see that joy isn't dependent upon what you acquire, but who you are in Christ.

Don't indulge your children and don't allow anyone else to spoil them either. Sit down with the grandparents and have a *come to Jesus* meeting with them. Grandparents usually don't intend to undermine the training of your children, but they can do it in a heartbeat if you let them give your kids whatever they want. Encourage grandparents to offer the kids love and support rather than video games and material stuff. Those intangible gifts are much more valuable than spoiling or spending, and they will help to reinforce your priorities with your kids.

The Starting Point

Do you live in a household filled with discontent? Do your kids hound and harangue you for everything they want? Do you feel yourself caving in to the pressure to make more, buy more, move up, live large?

You're not alone.

We are all bombarded with over a thousand ads every day. Marketing experts excel at making us feel dissatisfied. Your life is incomplete, and you're incompetent unless you drive the right car, live in the right neighborhood, and have the newest flat screen TV. You're conditioned to want, want, want.

No wonder we're filled with unfulfillment.

But you can change it.

You can teach your children self-control and contentment. And you can teach yourself as well.

Like most other principles that we try to pass on to our children, contentment must be modeled. Your children need to see and sense that you are happy and at peace with life as it is, not constantly striving for more. They need

Your children need to see and sense that you are happy and at peace with life as it is, not constantly striving for more.

to understand that real joy comes when we recognize God's gifts and open our hearts to share them with others.

There are simple ways to communicate those truths to your children, even when they're very young:

- "You are not always going to get something when we go to the store."
- "Yes, honey, I like those shoes, but remember, we're shopping for what we *need*, not what we *want*."
- "You have a lot of video games that you don't use. Is there someone you could give those to who would enjoy playing with them?"
- "Let's sort through our closets and give away the things we rarely wear."

Be intentional about teaching your children the difference between a want and a need. We *need* the basics of life, such as food, clothing, and shelter. We don't *need* designer jeans or hundred-dollar tennis shoes. We don't *need* a fifty-five-inch flat screen TV. Once we understand the difference, we can begin to move toward true contentment. In fact, once you and your kids grasp the concept of streamlining and simplifying, you may find that you're actually having fun living that way.

Teach your kids to express thanks for anything and everything— big stuff, little stuff, things they've always taken for granted.

Growing in Gratitude

One way to help your kids grow in contentment is to teach them to be grateful—even for something they didn't like or desire. If they don't say "thank you" for something, they don't get to keep the gift. It's good motivation. It impresses on them to be other-focused. It gives them a practical outworking of the biblical teaching that we should honor others above ourselves (Romans 12:10).

Beth does a great job of continually reinforcing the expectation of expressing genuine thanks. Years ago, she began teaching our kids why it's important. If someone cared enough about you and was willing to take the time, energy, and forethought to do or give something, then the appropriate response is to thank them.

When our kids received a gift, they were expected to write a brief thank-you note within the next couple of days. If they didn't do it, they couldn't play or get on the computer or watch television until it was done. For a six-year-old, an appropriate thank-you might be a one-sentence note with a picture drawn beside it. For a teenager, a paragraph or two.

Thank-you notes serve a number of purposes. They help foster gratitude, of course. But they also teach your children how to express themselves and how to open their hearts to the people God has put in their lives. And although we live in the electronic age, texts, tweets, and e-mails can't compare to the good old-fashioned handwritten letter. A real note, on real paper with a real envelope and a real overpriced stamp, is guaranteed to put a smile on the face of the one who blessed you.

Teach your kids to express thanks for anything and everything—big stuff, little stuff, things they've always taken for granted. In time it will become second nature to say, "Thank you"—to you, to others around them, and to God.

Whenever we eat together as a family, whether we're at home or away, everyone knows they're expected to express thanks to the person who made the meal or paid for it. There have been times when we've gone out to eat, and after dinner I will sit in the car and not start it. Invariably someone asks, "What are we waiting for?" At that instant everybody will quickly review in their own mind whether they've said, "Thanks for dinner."

The earlier you begin, the sooner thankfulness will become a habit that takes root in the lives of your children. As a parent, don't get upset if your children forget sometimes. I'm confident that their lineage is human. The end goal is not legalism or guilt trips, but developing a spirit of thankfulness in that young heart.

The Root of All Evil

When my brother and I were growing up, we had the kinds of arguments that probably sound familiar in your house as well:

"Dad, Jeff's on my side of the back seat. He crossed the invisible line."

"Mom! He's got more ice cream than me."

"Jeff got a bigger slice of pizza than I got!"

And my mom, tired of our discontent, would look at us and sigh and say, "Always wanting more."

What's the root of evil in the world? Stand on a sidewalk and ask a dozen people, and you'll probably get this answer most of the time: money is the root of all evil.

But that's not what the Bible says. First Timothy 6:10 tells us that "the love of money" is a root of all kinds of evil. And if we think about it, we understand all too well what that means.

The heart of the American culture beats for money and things. Most young people today have grown up with a sense of entitlement. Kids feel justified in having the newest iPhone, the best laptop, and more technological toys than a forty-year-old CEO. They nag and complain and wear their parents down until they get what they want. The economy is going down, while desires are still going up.

It's an impending head-on collision, and it's going to be a spectacular crash. Millions of kids with unrealistic expectations, and millions of parents drowning in debt and mortgaging their future so Johnny can have what he wants.

But we have to stop and ask ourselves: Where did Johnny get the idea that he can have what he wants when he wants it?

The problem with today's Christian family is our desire to *fit in* rather than *stand out*. Instead of saving for what we need, we borrow for what we want. Rather than being content with a ten-year-old Toyota that runs just fine, we covet the neighbor's brand-new Mercedes.

It's no wonder our kids feel entitled. We let the world's priorities dictate how we live and how we parent.

A variety of things can produce happiness in your life. If you get the dress at a great price, if your favorite team wins, if the home front is peaceful—then you are happy. But happiness is based on circumstances, and when the circumstances change, the good feeling dissipates like mist.

Joy is more than happiness. It comes from the inside. It goes beyond the excitement of the pay raise, the A on the test, or the first date with that special someone. Joy is lasting and rich. *It's not dependent on your possessions; it's derived from your purpose.* Joy runs deeper than happiness.

I like the way my friend Rick Atchley puts it: "Let's stop wearing ourselves out acquiring future landfill. Lasting joy doesn't come from stuff that doesn't last."[12]

When your family's "joy" is merely the by-product of constant acquisition, you cease to be a committed Christ follower and become a chameleon instead. You blend in and adapt to your surroundings. You become part of the culture . . . and therefore part of the problem.

But the Lord calls His followers to a countercultural lifestyle.

Comfort vs. Contentment

A first-century Roman proverb warns: "Money is like seawater: the more a man drinks, the thirstier he becomes." Now, I don't know if Jesus knew that saying—maybe He did. He certainly understood the principle, if His lifestyle is any indication. He kept it simple, trusted God, had what He needed, and didn't covet more.

Romans 12:2 instructs us, "Do not conform to the pattern of this world, but be transformed by the renewing of your mind" (NIV 2011). If that's not clear enough, listen to the way the J. B. Phillips version paraphrases that verse: "Don't let the world around you squeeze you into its own mould."

It's a challenge for us twenty-first-century Western Christians, who have so many creature comforts. Our lavish lifestyle chips away at our dependence upon God. The Holy Spirit may be called the Comforter, but we don't have much need to depend on His comfort. We're self-made. We're independent. We can take care of ourselves, thank you very much.

Author Francis Chan asks this question of American Christians: "Why would we need to experience the Comforter if our lives are already comfortable?"[13]

The problem is, the kind of comfort we find through a life of luxury doesn't offer the deeper level of contentment and joy found in a relationship with God. What the world gives is temporary and superficial, and it can vanish overnight, leaving us with nothing. But real contentment, as the apostle Paul discovered, isn't contingent on finances, status, or possessions:

> I have learned to be content whatever the circumstances. I know what it is to be in need, and I know what it is to have plenty. I have learned the secret of being content in any and every situation, whether well fed or hungry, whether living in plenty or in want. (Philippians 4:11–12)

And what's Paul's secret? "I can do all this through him [Christ] who gives me strength" (Philippians 4:13 NIV 2011). This imperfect servant had matured to the point that his contentment wasn't found in possessions; it was found in Christ.

Years ago, a small Albanian nun took the name Sister Mary Teresa and began working among the poorest of the poor in the slums of Calcutta. She washed the sores of lepers, nursed patients with tuberculosis, and gave hope and dignity to some of the forgotten of the world. For her work she was awarded the Pope John XXIII Peace Prize, the Nehru Prize for her promotion of international peace and understanding, and eventually the Nobel Peace Prize. She refused the $192,000 award, giving it instead to the poor people of India.

When Mother Teresa died at the age of eighty-seven, she reportedly left behind an estate that consisted of a prayer book and three saris.

And a world that was changed because she followed the call of God.

Now, there's nothing wrong with wealth. The Bible abounds with examples of wealthy and godly individuals—Abraham, David, Job, Nicodemus, Joseph of Arimethea, and Lydia, to name a few. But even though they knew prosperity, they still kept God as the priority. They used their position and possessions for the purpose of bringing glory to God.

If you've been blessed financially, then make certain you do the same.

The Generous Heart

A number of years ago, we bought a lot in a new neighborhood with the intention of paying it off and then building a new house there. During the time of construction, our family went on a mission trip to the Dominican Republic.

One night about a month before we were to move into the much-anticipated new home, I was praying with Sam. He was nine at the time. As I was turning the lights off, I noticed that he was fighting back tears. "What's wrong?" I asked.

"I wish . . . I wish that instead of moving into a new house, we could take that money and go back on another mission trip to the Dominican."

He was heartfelt. I was speechless. This was no joke, and in his mind it was a no-brainer. Why wouldn't we be willing to make such a trade?

I'm afraid I know why. Sam was only nine. He hadn't been jaded by the commercialism and materialism of our culture—yet. In his mind, a mission trip trumped a bigger bedroom and backyard. And although he was too young to understand all the factors that went into the decision, it was clear that he got Jesus' message: "It is more blessed to give than to receive" (Acts 20:35).

Generosity goes against the grain of our desire to stock-pile our stuff. Be grateful, be generous, and hold the things of this world loosely. When your children see you sharing with others, giving freely and anonymously to people in need, they'll absorb those lessons—and will probably amaze you with their generosity along the way.

Gratefulness leads to contentment, which leads to generosity, which produces joy.

May your children voluntarily pass up birthday gifts in order to help the less fortunate. May they wish for a mission trip rather than a bigger room.

May they be grateful. May they be generous. May they be joyful.

May they learn to be content, whether in plenty or in want.

And may they learn it from you.

7

"I've Got Your Back"

I knew immediately that this was going to be the most embarrassing moment of my life. The one I'd never live down. Seated next to my older brother in a crowded children's session at a large church convention, I prayed for God to take me to heaven or to open the floor and swallow me up.

When you're a very young boy, too much water and a too-small bladder make for a deadly combination. Especially in a too-long church meeting.

My mom's wardrobe choice for me that night wasn't helping matters: a pair of light gray slacks. Now, gray pants show every drop of water or . . . whatever. They provide absolutely no camouflage. There was no hiding the incriminating evidence.

Forced to throw myself on the mercy of my older brother, I whispered, "Jeff, I had an accident, and I need your help."

This was rather like serving up a hanging curve to Angels superstar slugger Albert Pujols or asking *X-Factor* judge Simon Cowell what he thinks of your singing. I braced myself for the laughter.

But it never came. Instead, he sat there surveying the situation and searching for a solution.

Then divine intervention occurred. Someone on the stage said, "Boys and girls, let's close our eyes and talk to God." Jeff and I looked at each other as if the Red Sea had been parted again. This was a miracle, a gift from God. So, with every head bowed and every eye closed, Jeff seized the moment. "Follow me."

He walked directly in front of me. I stayed close behind. Very close. This went beyond tailgating; it bordered on *back drafting* like a NASCAR driver. In perfect synchronized step we made our way down a crowded hallway. He sent me into a bathroom stall and instructed me to wait until he could locate Mom and Dad. Another miracle! He spotted them in the midst of thousands of adults in an auditorium, got them out of their session, and brought them to me.

The three of them assumed positions like blockers on a football field, one in front and one on each side. Like a human amoeba we choreographed our steps all the way around the convention center to a shuttle bus. Then back to our hotel for a change of clothes.

And finally we could laugh about it.

The laughter, you'll notice, was reserved for the private setting with the family. And the story wasn't revealed until many years later, when my mortifying experience was but a distant memory in the rearview mirror of life.

What should have been my most embarrassing moment instead became an unforgettable lesson on loyalty from loved ones.

Accidents will happen. My family understood. They knew how to extend grace instead of guilt, assurance instead of embarrassment. They would never expose me to public ridicule.

They had my back.

Lessons in Loyalty

Loyalty isn't taught as much as it's caught.

I've seen this principle at work so clearly in families with a special needs child. Everybody pulls together to undergird, encourage, and defend that individual. Nobody would dare crack a joke or make a face at the expense of that Down syndrome child, or they'd wish they hadn't. The anger of a lioness with a stolen cub is nothing compared to the fury of big brother when his kid sister is being made fun of.

But shouldn't that type of devotion be evident within *every* family? Shouldn't we all have unswerving allegiance to our loved ones? Siblings should never tolerate the mistreatment or ridicule of a family member.

Your children need to see that everybody's needs are special needs. When it comes to the family, you're a team. You defend one another. You stick up for one another.

Remember the family that refers to themselves as the "Turner Team"? The very name communicates family faithfulness and solidarity. When you refer to yourself as a team, you're saying that you're in this together. You have not only individual identities, but a collective identity as well.

How do you build a team? Well, you can promote allegiance by telling stories about your great-grandparents and ancestors on both sides of the family. You can share some positive accounts of loyalty and teamwork among aunts and uncles and grandparents. Kids need to hear of the legacy that's been left to them. If your children are young, you might tell them bedtime stories about their ancestors each Monday night. Call them "Links of Loyalty." Show them a chain and explain that the family name is only as strong as the weakest link.

My daughter Sadie babysits for the Richardson family—three kids under the age of five. One night the kids were watching a Disney movie, and one of the characters said something mean to another one.

The oldest child, Ella, let out a gasp.

Sadie turned to her and said, "Ella, would any of you say or do something like that to one another?"

Little Ella stared at Sadie in disbelief. "No way," she said. "We're *Richardsons*!"

Even at this early age, Ella realizes who she is and the distinctiveness of her family. There is a sense of family identity that runs deep.

Such a high expectation of devotion to one another will require repeated explanation to your toddlers, ongoing clarification to your kids, and constant reinforcement to your teens. But the effort is worth it, because in the future, the links of your family chain will not break under stress or pressure.

The Top Priority

In Luke 14, when crowds are following Jesus, He takes advantage of the large audience to make a point about our highest allegiance.

You may want to sit down for this one.

Jesus says, "If anyone comes to me and does not hate father and mother, wife and children, brothers and sisters—yes, even their own life—such a person cannot be my disciple" (Luke 14:26 NIV 2011).

It's a shocking verse. I can almost hear you protesting. "Whoa, Dave, what are you thinking? That is not the passage to include in the Faithful Families book series."

Isn't it? It's a pivotal principle. If you want to raise joyful, genuine Christian kids, you must be totally sold out for

Christ. So much so that the strong, positive feelings for your family (and even yourself) pale in comparison to your love for the Lord.

Jesus doesn't mean "hate" in the traditional sense. He's using hyperbole to stress that love for Him is to supersede any other love. Even back in the first century, Jesus knew that most people's name badges would list "Family" as their passion. But the first passion, the ultimate priority, ought to be our relationship with God.

This is a huge struggle for a lot of Christian parents. A Luke 14:26 loyalty means that if the soccer game is the same time as church, the team plays without your child. Loyalty to Jesus first means that if your only excuse for not going on a mission trip to serve the poor is that your kids would miss you, then you'd better dust off your passport.

Jesus is simply saying, "I want and deserve your unbending loyalty." He wants to be your top priority. And when you love Him first and best, love for your family and loyalty to them will follow naturally.

Sacred Moments

Do you ever wonder why the divorce rate is so high, why there are so many broken homes, out-of-control kids, and cynical grown-ups? We live in a society that could benefit from some lessons in loyalty.

Relationships can't survive on broken promises, unpaid debts, unreturned calls, or weak excuses. But relationships thrive in an environment of acceptance, transparency, trust, promises made, and promises kept.

Nothing will destroy a relationship quicker than a broken confidence. And nothing will build it like honoring the sacred moments of life.

Life is full of private and personal situations that shouldn't be shared outside the family circle. Teach your kids the meaning of confidentiality. Continually remind them that some conversations or embarrassing moments are private family matters that shouldn't be disclosed. Teach them to protect their siblings rather than ridicule them or rat them out to their friends.

Treat discipline issues of kids, and humiliating moments with their siblings, as sacred. The details stay in the home, and any other rebroadcast, retransmission, distribution, or exhibition of the event, without the express written consent of the parents, is strictly prohibited.

Translation: some stuff is private stuff. When those things happen, immediately remind the siblings, "We won't be talking about this outside the home because we love one another, and telling others won't help the situation. If your friends ask questions, you can just say, 'My brother made an unwise choice and can't play with us today.' Period."

This teaches kids what is fair game and what isn't. If they are ever in doubt, tell them to ask a parent first before saying anything. And if the parents aren't present, play it safe and choose silence first. There's probably a good reason they are uncertain—doubt can be a wise filter.

Teaching your children what stays private and what can go public will be an ongoing challenge. But if the Internet teaches us anything, it demonstrates how fast unsubstantiated gossip can go viral and how much damage it can do.

The older your kids get, the more dirt they have on you—but fortunately, the more you have on them too. Those numerous tales we could tell about one another breed loyalty rather than disclosure. My kids certainly have plenty of embarrassing stories based on my idiosyncrasies and multitude of mistakes, but those memories are locked away in mental vaults, never to be publicly revealed.

And that's the way I'd like to keep it.

Positive Pressure

Do you want to have a family where joy blows through and brings freshness to everyday life? Cultivate loyalty. Loyalty lubricates the hinges of your relationships and opens the windows and doors so that the Spirit can come in. Along with your family mission statement, it will give purpose and confidence to each member of your team.

Those
numerous
tales we could
tell about
one another
breed loyalty
rather than
disclosure.

One of the reasons we've had little drama in our home, thus far, is that our kids made wise choices and didn't toy with some of the temptations that can destroy and divide families. While they're not perfect, they are committed to the Lord and to our family.

When they were about nine or ten, I promised each of our kids that I would give them $500 when they turned eighteen if they were still a virgin, had never smoked a cigarette, and had never experimented with drugs or alcohol. Bribery? Maybe. But it's worked thus far.

Sam, of course, still has a year to go. He claims he's going to use the prize money to throw one wild birthday party. (I *think* he's joking.)

In a society that turns up its nose at the concept of delayed gratification, I believe it's wise to hang some carrots in front of your kids. Give them a goal to shoot for, and in the process, they'll be establishing habits that will serve them all their lives.

And I've discovered something else in the process: my daughters are rallying behind Sam, encouraging him and pulling for him to meet the expectation. They offer verbal support and suggestions to make it easier. They'd never dream of trying to undermine him.

They've got his back. They're rooting for his success.

Family loyalty could be described as *positive peer pressure*.

Now understand—at the time I made that pledge to my kids, I didn't have five hundred dollars. I didn't have fifty.

But through the years, God provided, and I'm confident He would do the same for your family.

To be honest, I would have mortgaged the house to honor that commitment to my kids. It's worth it to have the assurance that your teens are making wise choices. And I suspect you'd gladly do it, too, for the peace of mind that they are heading in the right direction.

Ironically, neither of my daughters, who have since reached that milestone, asked me for the money on their eighteenth birthday. Maybe they forgot. More likely, they realized that a firm foundation was worth more than the money. Either way, it was clear that they didn't do it for the cash. They stuck with the plan because of who they had become.

A large of sum of money looming in the future can be a great motivator when you're young. But along the way a higher purpose becomes the goal and helps kids avoid some of the typical teenage pitfalls. The girls have now been paid, and our son is still on track for his windfall.

And just for the record: Sam, we'll entertain your proposal about an *inflation adjustment* next spring!

In Your Corner

If you are serious about building family ties through faith, love, and laughter, then it must be evident to each family member that you are in one another's corner.

The home must become a safe haven for family members to retreat, to be themselves, and to know that they are accepted, defended, and protected.

Truth is, my older brother Jeff is still a little gun-shy when he's seated beside me and knows I've had too much water to drink. But even forty years later, loyalty still wins out over self-preservation or public ridicule.

Why? Because we're family.

Family's got your back.

And in my particular case . . . the front, too.

8

Word Power

When I was in high school, I began making a list of the odd, funny, and sometimes ridiculous things I heard from my mom and dad. When they became exasperated by my behavior, they came out with some pretty illogical statements. Maybe you've heard some of these from your parents. Maybe you've said them yourself.

"Be careful," my mom would say every time I picked up a toy. "You're gonna poke your eye out with that thing."

Now I could understand a bow and arrow set or a BB gun, but come on, Mom. It's a beach ball!

"Stop tattling on your brother," she would say, "or I'm going to *tell your father*!"

If I was talking too much at the dinner table, my dad would say, "Close your mouth and eat your food." I was never sure how it was possible to do both.

Or I'd come running inside and forget to shut the front door. From his La-Z-Boy recliner Dad would yell, "Boy, were you born in a barn?"

I've often wondered if Joseph ever said that when Jesus left the door open.

Joseph: "Boy, were you born in a barn?"

Jesus: "As a matter of fact, yes, I was."

Joseph: "Uhh, okay, just keep it open then."

My all-time favorite, though, had to be this one: I'd be watching television and my mom would come in. "Don't forget you've got to mow the lawn."

And, yes, I was taught immediate obedience. So I'd get up and head out the door.

"Where do you think you are going, barefoot?" Mom would say.

"I think I'm going to mow the lawn. You asked me to mow the lawn."

"You are *not* going to mow the lawn barefoot."

"Why not?"

"That lawn mower will cut your legs off."

Now, granted, a lawn mower could do some serious damage. It might cut your feet off, but not your legs. It was a physical impossibility. I told her so.

And then came the final word: "Okay, okay, Mr. Smart Guy, go on out there! Mow the lawn barefoot. But when that lawn mower cuts your legs off, don't come running to me!"

No doubt my kids have gotten a good laugh out of some of my comments as well. It's payback for the chuckles I got at my parents' expense. The expressions may be funny, but the intention is sound. Warning, teaching, training, social development—regardless of the word choice, the purpose comes through. Parents mean well.

At least most of the time.

Words will Never Hurt Me?

S ticks and stones may break my bones, but words will never hurt me."

That may be the biggest lie ever foisted on children. Words hurt. A broken bone will heal. But sometimes the wounds from cruel words linger for decades.

Sometime ago I was on a retreat with my staff. Together we shared some of the more painful and damaging comments that came from our parents. I was at a loss to come up with one, but plenty of people there struggled to narrow down their choices.

If the previous list made you laugh, these might make you cry. They are real. They are painful. They're like a ticking hand grenade lobbed from parent to child.

- "You'll never get a date if you don't lose that weight."
- "You can't do anything right. I wish I'd never had you."

- "You're so dumb, boy; step aside, I'll do it."
- "Too bad you're not as pretty as your sister."
- "Face it, you will never amount to anything!"

Some of those comments dated back more than half a century, but the effect was as fresh and raw as if the words had been uttered yesterday.

Forgiven? Perhaps.

Forgotten? Never.

Climate Control

As parents, we are responsible for the verbal climate in our families. It's up to us to create situations and settings where family members say uplifting and affirming comments to one another rather than words that are demeaning and hurtful. In the car, around the dinner table, in all sorts of situations in everyday life, words can cut and scar, or they can mend and heal.

Take an interest in one another's lives. Applaud those in your family whose words lift up others. Positivity generates joy. Raise your kids to care about their siblings and genuinely celebrate with one another. Teach them from the time they are toddlers how to bestow blessings with their words rather than barbs.

Teach them from the time they are toddlers how to bestow blessings with their words.

The Bible minces no words of its own in driving home encouragement and warning when it comes to the words we say. Here are just a few:

- "If anyone considers himself religious and yet does not keep a tight rein on his tongue, he deceives himself and his religion is worthless" (James 1:26).
- "He who guards his lips guards his life, but he who speaks rashly will come to ruin" (Proverbs 13:3).
- "Let your conversation be always full of grace" (Colossians 4:6).

Your efforts coupled with God's blessings can transform a home.

So, what kind of words do we need to speak?

Truthful Words

Train your children to tell the truth and teach them why it is so important. Lies undermine trust, destroy relationships, and damage one's reputation both in the family and beyond. Help your children understand that when they are truthful, they reflect their heavenly Father.

Your children need to learn the wisdom of telling the truth the first time. When Christians open their mouths, the only thing that should come out is truth.

Besides, the truth will always come out in the end, so the sooner the better.

Positive Words

I f you've got young children, you already know that they will whine if they think whining will get them what they want. Can you blame them?

When you give in to whining, you're teaching them that this is an acceptable method for getting their way. You're rewarding immaturity and thus enabling it. Parenting then becomes more difficult, because every decision becomes a debate.

Establish your home as a *No Whining Zone*. Teach your kids that it's unacceptable behavior. It's negative, it's unattractive—and it doesn't work. And then, seriously, do not cave in when your kids whine!

Years ago when Savannah, our firstborn, was about four, she came into the kitchen and started asking for something with a whiny voice. Beth was very matter-of-fact and said, "Savannah, I can't understand you when you speak like that. Go to your room and come back when you can talk to me in a big girl voice."

Beth didn't rake Savannah over the coals, nor did she make a big deal out of it. Beth showed no drama, she just calmly stated the expectation. To our surprise, Savannah learned the lesson instantly; the behavior was never repeated. Now, that's the exception and not the norm. But there's a lesson for us as parents, too: be careful what you tolerate, because it will become a habit.

Instead of rewarding negativity by giving in to it, catch your kids and their friends in the act of saying something positive—and then reward them. For instance, each morning when Beth used to drive car pool, she would tell the kids, "Find someone to encourage today."

In the afternoon when our children and the neighborhood kids would get back in the car, she would say, "Okay, tell me how you encouraged someone today." She kept an Encouragement Jar in our minivan with treats in it. An encouraging comment gained you access to the jar. That daily routine sent a message to all of those kids that encouragement should become as natural as breathing.

Biblical Words

Sometimes as parents we get focused on what works, but we need to remember that the higher motivation is to correlate life situations with Scripture. It is one of the best ways to influence the words our children say.

Recently I was at lunch with a couple and their two young children—Carson, who is seven, and Caroline, who's six. Halfway through the meal, their father Darren asked, "Would you kids like to tell Mr. Stone your memory verses?"

I listened while each of them rattled off three lengthy verses. The passage was Ephesians 6:1–3: "Children, obey your parents in the Lord, for this is right. 'Honor your father and mother'—which is the first commandment with a promise—'so that it may go well with you and that you may enjoy long life on the earth.'"

I'm not sure what struck me more, the ability of the youngsters to memorize or the parents' choice of passages. Out of all the verses in the Bible, Darren and Amanda picked a passage that would impress God's directives on their children very early in life.

Wise choice.

Loving Words

I f you've been married for any length of time, you've probably noticed the way some couples speak critically to each other. Their conversations with the "love of their life" could be described as condescending, patronizing, and demeaning—anything but loving.

Write it down, take it to the bank: Their kids will speak to one another the same way their parents do. Children parrot their parents . . . so speak kind and affirming words to your spouse.

Not too long ago in our church's new-member orientation, each person was sharing why they came to Southeast Christian for the first time. One woman said, "Well, at work my cubicle is right outside the office of a man who is a member here. And each day I would overhear the tone and the way he spoke to his wife and kids on the telephone. That is what attracted me to this church."

Never underestimate the power of your words in or outside your home.

If you are serious about your family being a joyful, distinctive family, then raise the bar of expectation for the way you talk to one another. We make all sorts of excuses for why our kids talk hatefully to their siblings and disrespectfully to their parents. We wouldn't allow them to speak to their best friend that way or to any other adult. Why should the expectation be lower for loved ones?

When you raise the bar, you increase the degree of loyalty within the family. You send a clear message to others that the members of this family respect and love one another, and that our words reflect that love through kindness, compassion, and thoughtfulness.

The way we talk to one another can increase our joy instead of stealing it.

If you are serious about your family being a joyful, distinctive family, then raise the bar of expectation for the way you talk to one another.

Encouraging Words

L et's face it, picking on, tearing down, and making fun come all too naturally for some people. When it comes to what you have to say to your family, you can either be on the demolition team or the construction crew.

"Reckless words pierce like a sword," Proverbs tells us, "but the tongue of the wise brings healing" (Proverbs 12:18–19). We're called to speak encouraging words that heal and strengthen, rather than negative words that wound and discourage.

When Sadie was four years old, she had been disciplined for some wrongdoing. Through her tears she looked at me and said, "You are the meanest daddy *in the whole world*!"

Fortunately, her seven-year-old sister Savannah intervened on my behalf. She said, "Sadie, you shouldn't say that. It would be nicer if you said he's the meanest daddy *in America*." Thanks so much for your help, Savannah. . . .

Evidently at the time, we were working with Savannah on saying encouraging words. In hindsight I guess we also should have been working on it with Sadie!

A number of years ago, evangelist Bill Glass addressed a group of a thousand prison inmates. He asked them this question: "How many of you had parents who told you that one day you'd end up in prison?" Nearly every one of the inmates raised his hand.[14]

We shouldn't be surprised. What we say to our children is prophetic, for better or worse. They live up to the belief we have in them.

Maybe you had a dysfunctional family and your parents didn't speak affectionately you. Maybe you grew up with negative or demeaning language. Maybe you were told you were stupid or incompetent or would never amount to anything. Maybe you believed it.

It's time to break the cycle. You have the opportunity to unleash potential or squelch it. Solomon reminds us, "The tongue has the power of life and death" (Proverbs 18:21).

Please don't mistake encouragement for a cheap imitation of the real thing. Flattery is what you'd say to someone's face, but you wouldn't say behind their back. Gossip is what you'd say behind their back, but you wouldn't say to their face. Encouragement comes from the heart and is genuine. It only serves its purpose if you mean it and it's true. A child can sense phoniness in a heartbeat.

Think about it. How would your children describe the way you speak to them?

The way you speak can affect your children now and for all their lives. So choose your words carefully.

Dr. Gary Chapman, in his book *The Five Love Languages*, identifies five different ways that individuals receive love. One of those love languages is Words of Affirmation.[15] If you have a child who is wired that way, then as a parent you need to speak affirming words frequently.

My son Sam is like that. I remember when he was about four years old and trying to putt a golf ball all the way down the driveway. As he was getting ready to hit the ball, he stopped and looked up at me and said, "Daddy, I'll hit. You cheer."

Unknowingly he was telling me how he most naturally receives love. If you learn how to affirm your children when they're young, it becomes easier for them to feel loved throughout their childhood and adolescence by your words of praise—regardless of their love language.

Clean Words

My parents didn't use profanity. They monitored what we watched on television. They protected the home environment. As a result, dirty language is foreign to me—and it's as unwelcome as cigar smoke in a neonatal unit. It doesn't belong.

In recent years, profanity and vulgarity have become everyday vocabulary, so commonplace that they barely register a blip on society's emotional radar screen. The vulgarity of today's youth has escalated in direct proportion to the permissiveness of parents. Vile language has become a way of life.

But such language is a poison in the home. If your kids have been around friends who use vulgar language, you'll know it soon enough. It rubs off. It doesn't take long to surface. Our little angels will test the boundaries even if they hurt someone in the process.

The Bible is clear about God's expectation for the language that comes out of our mouths:

- "Nor should there be obscenity, foolish talk or coarse joking, which are out of place, but rather thanksgiving" (Ephesians 5:4).
- "But now you must also rid yourselves of all such things as these: anger, rage, malice, slander, and filthy language from your lips" (Colossians 3:8).
- "Do not let any unwholesome talk come out of your mouths, but only what is helpful for building others up according to their needs, that it may benefit those who listen" (Ephesians 4:29).

Keep it clean. Keep it pure. Your home will be a kinder, more peaceful place because of the words you use—and those you avoid.

Urgent Words

Some of you may be thinking, "This doesn't come naturally to me." Perhaps your parents had foul mouths, your dad never said he loved you, or you are aware that you use your tongue more as a weapon than a tool of encouragement.

You can change. Your family can change. You can be a model in this discipline. What if you and your family became known as true encouragers? What if people consistently sought your family out because they knew your conversation would lift their spirits? What if your spouse and your kids heard you expressing words of love and commitment, of faith and encouragement, every single day? How would that change your world?

John Trent and Gary Smalley, in their bestselling book *The Blessing*, remind us: "When it comes to verbal encouragement, the most common mistake that parents make is saying, 'I'll tell them tomorrow.' "[16]

How about today? How about *now*? Take a minute and go tell each of your children, one-on-one, what you appreciate about them and that you love them. Tell your husband or wife. It may feel awkward at first if you aren't used to expressing yourself this way. Your kids may even laugh it off, but they will come to appreciate it. In fact, in time, they may say those same words to you.

Tell each of your children, one-on-one, what you appreciate about them and that you love them.

Twelve Godly Words

Years ago Cliff Barrows was an associate to Billy Graham in his crusades around the world. Barrows has been quoted as saying, "These are the twelve most important words in any close relationship: I was wrong. I am sorry. Please forgive me. I love you."

My mentor Bob Russell adds: "If you haven't spoken those twelve words to your spouse recently, there are three others that can quickly make up for them: Let's eat out."

Whether you go out to dinner or not, those dozen words can breathe life and joy into your family. Look at what is communicated by each phrase: confession, repentance, forgiveness, and love.

And the greatest of these is love.

9

Servant Power

There I was, in Kenya, Africa, sprawled across a cheap motel mattress, sick as a dog, staring at the ceiling. My stomach felt like Jell-O® on a Ferris wheel, and the prospect of spending the next twenty-two hours on a plane didn't help. My suitcase, that should have already been taken to the loading area, still sat at the foot of the bed, mocking me in my hour of affliction.

Just then a knock came at the door. I opened it to find Olivia, the teenage daughter of Kurt and Kristen Sauder, standing there. "Mr. Stone, I know you're not feeling well. Would you like me to take your bag down to the bus?"

"No, that's okay, but thanks so much for offering," I said, trying to use my big-boy voice instead of whimpering.

I closed the door and groaned my way back to the bed. A couple of minutes later, there was another knock. This time it was Drew Sauder. "Mr. Stone, would you like me to take your bag down to the bus?"

Even in my moment of misery, I was capable of sizing up the situation. I resigned. "Yes, that would be great. Thanks so much, Drew."

Knowing that Kurt and Kristen had *four* children, I decided to prop the door open at this point. They didn't disappoint. The parade continued right on schedule.

Soon eleven-year-old Ellie Sauder passed by and asked if I needed help with my bag. I said, "Thanks, but your brother already got it." When her sister Ivy came past a few minutes later, I answered her before she even had a chance to ask the question.

And now I had something new to ponder other than my restless stomach. My mind was asking the same question yours is: How does that happen?

How do four kids between the ages of eleven and eighteen willingly volunteer to serve, without any prompting from their parents?

Here's a clue: They all share the same last name.

Service is second nature to the Sauder family. They derive great joy from their random acts of kindness.

In the New Testament we are challenged to put our faith into action. James wrote this:

> "Suppose a brother or a sister is without clothes
> and daily food. If one of you says to them, 'Go in

peace; keep warm and well fed,' but does nothing about their physical needs, what good is it? In the same way, faith by itself, if it is not accompanied by action, is dead." (James 2:15–17)

A faith that is alive is concerned about the needs of others.

More Than Words Can Say

In the previous chapter, we considered the power of words—their significance and their effect upon others for good or ill. Unfortunately, we live in a culture where words don't mean much. A life filled with broken promises can cause us to become cynical.

- Your coworker says, "You'll be the first one I call if I get an extra ticket."
- Your client says, "The check is in the mail."
- Your child says, "I'll never ever do that again."

Time will tell if those are simply words or if they are backed up by actions. Instead of accepting someone's word, just wait and see. Actions speak louder than words. Life service means more than lip service.

Jesus Himself stressed this in the Sermon on the Mount: "Not everyone who *says* to me, 'Lord, Lord,' will enter the kingdom of heaven, but only the one who *does* the will of my Father who is in heaven" (Matthew 7:21 NIV 2011, italics mine).

There is a drastic difference between saying and doing. Jesus was the example in both words and actions. He spoke the truth in love, and He served anyone who was in need.

That's a combination that could transform the dynamics of any family.

Good–Better–Best

When we were raising our kids, we'd motivate them with the Good–Better–Best principle. It became a teaching method that they could apply to any situation they encountered, regardless of their age. Basically it both applauded and stretched them.

On your way to a friend's house for dinner, for example, you might coach your eight-year-old like this: "When you've finished eating, if you say, 'May I be excused?' that would be *good*. But if you were to say, 'Thank you for dinner. I really liked the chicken. May I be excused?' then that would be *better*. And if you were to say, 'Thank you for the dinner. I really liked the chicken. Do you need any help cleaning up?' then that would be the *best*."

It's a method designed to continually raise the bar and help your children learn how to improve. On your way home, you can praise them on a job well done.

Part of your child's success will depend on your preparation. If before you go into a setting, you say, "Tonight let's work on being a servant," you can bring it to the forefront of their mind. If you target the heart first, then right behavior becomes a natural outgrowth.

Perhaps your ten-year-old rolls her eyes and gets huffy when you ask her to take her clean laundry upstairs and put it in her dresser. That gives you the chance to say to her, "What would be a better way to respond next time?"

- *Good* would be to have a positive attitude—with no eyeball rolling.
- *Better* would be for her to take the clean clothes upstairs and put them away without being asked.
- *Best* would be to volunteer to help fold clothes when she sees Mom or Dad getting the laundry out of the dryer.

Parenting is an ongoing opportunity for stretching and maturing your children.

Making a Difference

Little Ella Cordrey was only four when that massive earthquake rocked Haiti. Although her home was fifteen hundred miles away, she wanted to help. On her own she came up with an idea of making and selling cupcakes . . . and all the money would go to a Haiti Relief Fund. So she started with her sidewalk stand and made a few sales. But then a local television station heard about Ella's desire, and they did a story on her idea. In the end, she raised over $1,400. Other neighborhood kids were so inspired by young Ella that several came and emptied their entire piggy banks.

Now, as much as we may applaud Ella, you and I both know that her parents, Ronnie and Tish, had a lot to do with it. They had already planted seeds of serving in her young life. And they worked hard to make her idea possible. Together the family baked over six hundred cupcakes in four days.

The Cordreys give us a great model for teaching servanthood. The earlier you develop the discipline of service in your family, the less it will seem like a chore. Allow your kids to come up with their own ideas of how to serve others. Permit them to take ownership of the project. Then work together as a team to make it a reality.

In his classic book *Celebration of Discipline*, Richard Foster cuts to the heart of what it means to truly be a servant:

> We must see the difference between choosing to serve and choosing to be a servant. When we choose to serve, we are still in charge. We decide whom we will serve and when we will serve. . . . But when we choose to be a servant, we give up the

The earlier you develop the discipline of service in your family, the less it will seem like a chore.

right to be in charge . . . we surrender the right to decide who and when we will serve. We become available and vulnerable.[17]

That's our goal as Christian parents: to raise servants, and not just kids who choose to serve.

Serving up Memories

On several occasions we have taken dinner to a group of homeless people in Louisville and had picnics with them at their campsite. In time they have become our friends and the focus of our prayers. Our entire family went to bless them, and yet each time we drove away, we were the ones who had been blessed. Some of those prayer circles with our family and our homeless friends are indelibly etched in our minds.

When you serve with your family, you make memories that will last forever. Those opportunities near and far, taught our family to be more tender-hearted, gracious, and generous. We all were forced out of our comfort zones—and we became better individuals and a closer family because of it.

We also got some of our greatest laughs.

After Hurricane Katrina, our family went down to the Mississippi Gulf Coast with a mission group from our church. We spent Thanksgiving with people who had lost everything. We helped run a free clothing store and a food warehouse. We also served seven hundred people three meals a day, from a makeshift kitchen in a parking lot.

Now, cooking for hundreds outdoors wasn't going to win any taste tests, nor did it set any records for sanitation ratings. Beth loved ministering to the people, but the food didn't appeal much to her, and she hardly ate at all.

On the third night, she suggested we leave the mission and drive thirty minutes away to an Applebees® restaurant. I have to admit, it didn't take a lot of arm-twisting for the other four of us to acquiesce. We were practically halfway there before we got the car doors shut.

Later that night, as the parking-lot meal was ending and the cleanup was starting, we arrived at the tent, back from our secret mission. Without a word to anyone, we slid into our places and started cleaning plates and washing dishes. The man who was in charge of the whole mission project passed Beth and said, "Boy, it was a great meal tonight, wasn't it?"

"Yes," Beth honestly replied, "it was the best meal of the week!"

We all thought her comment was hilarious, and, true to form in our family, we wasted no time in raking her over the coals for it. We laughed for weeks over her quick wit—and the truth of her statement.

To this day, that week in Mississippi is still our most memorable Thanksgiving. And we'll never forget the "best meal of the week"!

Honoring Others

When we think of serving, we usually think of work—some physical or tangible action, an outward labor. But sometimes serving is simply the act of honoring others above yourself. It may be as simple as listening instead of talking, or leaning in instead of spouting off.

Years ago we had a couple of special guests in our home. After spending two hours with one of them, my kids came away thinking how fascinating and special this person was. But the next month, when they spent two hours with another well-known public figure, my kids walked away from the experience feeling like *they* were fascinating and special.

The contrast is significant. One talked about all of his own personal accomplishments, while the other took an interest in drawing information out of our children. My kids still have a relationship with the second individual; we're not certain the first one even recalls that we have children.

That stark contrast became a practical life lesson for our kids. They began to notice the difference between selfishness and selflessness, and it taught them to make certain they took a genuine interest in others.

Sometimes serving is simply the act of honoring others above yourself.

Pure Hearts and Filthy Feet

I am the greatest."

It's the famous, now-iconic line of boxing champion Muhammad Ali. But he wasn't the first to think it. Jesus' disciples got into that argument as well—who was the greatest in the kingdom of God, who would sit beside Jesus in the world to come. They quibbled about status while Jesus talked about servanthood.

Finally, in John 13, Jesus chooses another teaching method. Evidently His previous speeches hadn't motivated His peeps toward humility and service. So the night of His betrayal, at the Passover meal we refer to as the Last Supper, Jesus abandons words and puts servanthood into action. He gets up from the meal, grabs a towel and a basin of water. One by one, foot by foot, callus by callus, the Master begins to wash and dry the filthy feet of His followers.

Here's the CliffsNotes version of His lesson: the greatest will be the servant of all.

When Jesus wanted to teach His disciples a lesson on life, the Miracle Worker got down on His knees. And then He said, "Do you understand what I have done for you? . . . Now that I, your Lord and Teacher, have washed your feet, you also should wash one another's feet. I have set you an example that you should do as I have done for you" (John 13:12, 15–16).

Did you catch it? He concludes the object lesson by adding this phrase, "Now that you know these things, you will be blessed if you *do* them" (John 13:17 NIV 2011, italics mine).

- It's *good* to see Jesus' example of serving.
- It's *better* to understand the call to servanthood.
- But it's *best* if you do it.

And the rest of the New Testament bears witness that this time the object lesson stuck with the disciples. They went on to pour their lives out in selfless service.

Service with a Smile

So how does *service* play out in our culture today?

- It's the mom who stays up late to help her child finish the school project he postponed until the last minute.
- It's the family who does the yard work at the home of an elderly person.
- It's the husband who hears the baby cry in the middle of the night and, instead of pretending to be asleep, gets up with the baby so his wife can rest. (And then

doesn't make a big deal of it the next morning!)
- It's the older brother who helps his younger brother do his chores so that they can both start playing sooner.

In the kingdom of God there is no ladder of greatness to climb, no spiritual one-upmanship, no humility trophies. "If anyone gives even a cup of cold water to one of these little ones because he is my disciple, I tell you the truth, he will certainly not lose his reward" (Matthew 10:42).

In the church, in the body of Christ, you will never ascend to any position higher than that of a servant. According to God's economy of things, that's the top of the heap. "For even the Son of Man did not come to be served, but to serve, and to give his life as a ransom for many" (Mark 10:45).

Keeping Things in Perspective

Service is a disarming discipline. When your family places the spotlight on others, the result is a contagious joy that permeates your family.

My preacher friend Carl Kuhl IV shares a time when he began to understand the value of serving others:

It was the Saturday before Thanksgiving. I was fifteen. It was a cold, rainy day, the kind of day that

When your family places the spotlight on others, the result is a contagious joy that permeates your family.

made you just want to stay inside. And the four of us kids were all getting on one another's nerves, pestering and aggravating one another.

Well, my mom had signed us up to take a Thanksgiving basket to a less fortunate family. We didn't want to go. But Dad put his foot down, and we all got in the car.

The air in the car was thick with tension. Dad got lost trying to find this home in a poor part of town. When we finally arrived, all six of us reluctantly plodded up to the door of this little shotgun house. A woman opened it, peeked out with one eye, and demanded, "Who are you?"

Mom explained that we were from a local church and had brought her food for Thanksgiving. The woman opened the door and let us in. She was in her pajamas. It appeared she hadn't showered in days.

Mom showed her what we'd brought and how to cook it: instant potatoes, canned vegetables, Stove Top stuffing. All stuff that in our nice home would have made for the worst Thanksgiving ever. But not for her. She couldn't stop weeping and thanking us.

There wasn't room for us to sit anywhere. So after a short visit, we excused ourselves. She gave each of us a big bear hug.

When we got back in the car, there wasn't any bickering or fighting over where my space ended and yours began. No pride. No sarcasm. Just silence. We finally realized that selfishness had been driving all of our emotions. But when our family took an hour to show someone the love of God, our selfishness turned into thankfulness.[18]

When service emerges, selfishness evaporates.

Random Acts of Kindness?

Remember the Sauders, whose kids all offered to carry my suitcase in Kenya? Earlier I said, "They derive joy from their random acts of kindness." But I was wrong. What the Sauders did in Kenya, what they do every single day, is not the least bit random—it's purposeful.

Let me remind you of the Sauders' family mission statement: *We exist to love and honor Jesus Christ by living for His kingdom and letting our light shine so that others will be fully devoted to Him.*

Now it makes sense. From their vantage point, it was quite natural to offer help to the queasy-stomached man who couldn't get his suitcase down to the bus.

It's who they are; it's what they do.

They know the power of serving. They understand that the last will be first, and the least will be greatest, and that being like Jesus means washing feet and hauling luggage.

They're just letting their light shine.

May it shine forever—in them, in you, and in all of us.

10

Plotting for Joy

I t's malignant."

The doctor's words rocked everyone in the waiting room. We might have suspected it, but *hearing* the diagnosis spoken out loud gave the results of the biopsy an uncomfortable air of finality.

Cancer. The word hung in the air like acrid smoke. I sat beside the family for a while, then stepped into a hallway to phone my parents.

Within seconds, both my parents were on the line. "What did the doctors find out?"

I couldn't speak. Nothing would come out of my mouth.

After about ten seconds of silence, my mom began to cry. "Oh no, it's bad, isn't it?"

I finally choked out the news. "It's cancer—but the doctors are extremely optimistic."

This wasn't just a member of my church.

It wasn't just a friend.

This was my twenty-one-year-old son-in-law, Patrick.

Six months before, our nineteen-year-old daughter Savannah had exchanged vows of commitment with him—for better or worse, for richer, for poorer, in sickness and in health. At that moment, this scenario was the furthest thing from anyone's mind.

They were young—some might say too young. But they loved God and they loved each other, and the Lord had given Beth and me peace about the marriage. We gave them our blessing and full support. And now the doctors had discovered a tumor the size of a grapefruit. Patrick was diagnosed with Hodgkin's lymphoma.

Plotting for Your Joy

I n all the setbacks of your life as a believer," John Piper says, "God is plotting for your joy."[19]

Sometimes it's hard to see the plan. The next few months were filled with question marks, chemotherapy, and radiation treatments. Through it all, Patrick and Savannah leaned on the Lord and their family. Truth is, they did better than the rest of us! Their spiritual maturity and acceptance of God's will inspired us all. They had peace and joy in the midst of this storm.

"In all the setbacks of your life as a believer," John Piper says, "God is plotting for your joy."

Beth was amazed at the strength and joy Savannah was displaying. One day she said, "You do know it's okay to have a bad day sometimes."

Savannah smiled back. "Yes, I know that."

And then she went on lifting the spirits of everyone else.

Watching Patrick deal with adversity for those months became a real-life demonstration that joy isn't based on circumstances. It comes from who you know and whose you are.

When your hair is falling out in clumps at the age of twenty-one . . .

When you have to drop out of college in the middle of a semester . . .

When you are uncertain if the treatments you're receiving might make you sterile and you don't yet have any children . . .

But you *still have joy* . . .

Then the only explanation is that it's coming from God's Spirit residing in you.

We Do Joy

In the very first chapter of this book I said that our day-to-day attitudes with our families grow out of an internal relationship with Jesus, not the external circumstances of life. And so no matter what happens *to* us, abundant life is what can happen *in* us.

What is your family's reaction when you receive bad news? There's sadness, disappointment, hurt, sometimes anger. You wouldn't be human if those weren't part of the initial reaction. But we can learn to be joyful in the midst of the adversity.

Paul had learned to be content in any and every situation (Philippians 4:12) because his overriding goal in life was to know Christ. Everything else flowed from that pursuit. That relationship changes how we view sadness and suffering, setbacks and sickness.

A couple of years ago someone gave us a large, handmade card that they had made and framed. At the top it read *The Stones*. Beside it was a picture of a home. The words beneath it described what occurred inside those four walls. It read:

IN THIS HOME . . .
We do second chances.
We do grace.
We do real.
We do mistakes.
We do "I'm sorrys."
We do LOUD really well.
We do hugs.
We do family.
We do love.

I hope that's an accurate description of your family. Those are some pretty significant ingredients if you are serious about building family ties. Beliefs shape behavior. Attitudes affect actions. Character controls conversations. Joy flourishes when our focus is on purpose rather than possessions.

Maybe you have a different list, tailor-made for your family. Post it on your refrigerator. Frame it and hang it on a prominent wall for all to see.

Give yourself a reminder of what's really important.

Someday Is Sooner Than You Think

I f you have infants or toddlers, you think, "Someday they'll be out of diapers. Someday they'll sleep through the night." If you have teenagers, you think, "Someday *we'll* sleep through the night."

But someday will come sooner than you think.

If you want to have a home that's marked by peace and joy and family togetherness, you have to take to heart the expectation of being a positive and purposeful parent. You have to start now.

You may think you've got all this time. Trust me, you don't. Someday they'll leave home, and it will happen in a heartbeat, long before you're ready for it.

If you think it will be difficult for you to release your children, can I let you in on a secret? It's a lot easier when you put into practice the lessons of this book. If your home has a joyful climate, you won't need to beg them to keep in touch.

Bob Benson wrote these wise words:

> Do you want to hold on to your kids? Then let go. Laugh with them, cry with them, rejoice with them, and dream with them. But let go of them. Then when they come down the driveway to see you, you can know that the only reason they are coming is because they want to see you. And you will begin to realize the deep joy that comes from having what you were willing to turn loose.[20]

The Longer View

Patrick did have cancer, and the months of chemotherapy and radiation were difficult. Fast forward two years: he's in full remission, he's preaching in the Fort Worth area, and doing extremely well. And thanks to his bout with cancer, he's a more compassionate and joyful pastor today than he ever would have been.

That's a tribute to Patrick . . . but please don't miss this. It's an even greater tribute to Patrick's *parents*, Dan and Rita. They raised their son to focus on Christ, rather than circumstances and to find joy in the midst of adversity with faith, love, and laughter.

What's more, the legacy of joy goes on. As this book is being written, Patrick and Savannah are expecting their first child. My first grandchild.

All along, God was plotting for their joy.

And I have good news. He's plotting for yours as well.

You and your family *will* face adversity—times when the twists and turns of life threaten to drain the joy from your heart. You may be in one of those valleys right now. You may think there's no earthly way your family can find joy and fulfillment in the face of those trials.

You're right. There is no earthly way.

But there's a heavenly way.

People without Jesus take a short-term view when they encounter trials, because the world is all they have to live for. But the Christian has a long-term view, an eternal perspective. Two thousand years ago on a Friday, things looked really bad. But on Sunday, Jesus walked out of His own grave, teaching us an unforgettable lesson about suffering and joy, about death and life.

That reality makes all the difference in the way you and your family can live each and every day. Joy prevails, even if the stock market slides, your job is downsized, your heart is broken, or the tumor is malignant.

Abundant life is not what happens to us, but what happens *in* us. It all comes back to you and your attitude.

No matter what life looks like on the outside, God is behind the scenes, plotting joy on your behalf. "He who began a good work in you will carry it on to completion until the day of Christ Jesus" (Philippians 1:6).

There is no family situation so dire that God cannot intervene. No dynamic too dysfunctional, no past too painful, no depression too deep.

The joyful Christian family doesn't belong on the endangered species list. It can make a comeback; its influence can be widespread and revolutionary.

And it can start with *you* . . . with *your family*. You can be an agent of transformation. First in your home. Then your neighborhood. Your church. Your community. And beyond.

Yes, you.

With faith, love, and laughter, you have all you need to build a family that can change the world.

Beginning today.

Also from Dave Stone

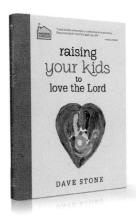
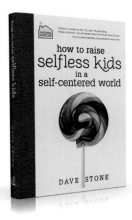

Please share how *Building Family Ties with Faith, Love & Laughter* has impacted your family:

Website: PastorDaveStone.com
Facebook: Facebook.com/FaithfulFamilies
Twitter: @TheFaithfulFam
Twitter: @DaveStone920

NOTES

1. Lewis Carroll, *Alice's Adventures in Wonderland* (New York: Macmillan, 1920), 89–90.

2. Max Lucado, *When God Whispers Your Name* (Dallas: Word, 1994), 34.

3. Conversation with Susan St. Clair, July 27, 2011. *Blending by the Book*, co-authored with husband, Lance (Growing Families International, Louisiana, MO).

4. Harry Emerson Fosdick, *Riverside Sermons* (New York: Harper and Brothers, 1958), 85.

5. Reuters News Service and CBS radio news, November 15, 2000.

6. Vance Havner, from "Sheep and Wolves," cited at http://www.friendsofvancehavner.org.

7. Tweeted at @RickAtchley on August 31, 2011.

8. Nancy Gibbs, "The Magic of the Family Meal," *Time*, 6-12-06, 51–56.

9. http://www.hazelden.org/web/public/prev51114.

10. http://www.webmd.com/parenting/news/20100208/less-tv-more-family-dinners-fight-childhood-obesity.

11. Cited in James Dobson's book *Bringing Up Boys* and credited to Andrew T. McLaughlin, "Family Dinners Provide Food for Thought As Well," *Boston Herald*, 14 March 1996.

12. Tweeted @RickAtchley, September 14, 2011.

13. Francis Chan, with Danae Yankowski, *Forgotten God: Revising Our Tragic Neglect of the Holy Spirit* (Colorado Springs: David C. Cook, 2009), 107.

14. Bill Glass, Champions for Life, Dallas, TX.

15. Gary Chapman, *The Five Love Languages: How to Express Heartfelt Commitment to Your Mate* (Chicago: Northfield, 1995).

16. Gary Smalley and John Trent, *The Blessing* (Nashville: Nelson, 2004), 57.

17. Richard Foster, *Celebration of Discipline: The Path to Spiritual Growth* (San Francisco: Harper & Row, 1998), 132.

18. On October 20, 2011, Carl Kuhl IV e-mailed me this personal story from his family's life. It is shared with his permission.

19. John Piper, "Ruth: The Best Is Yet to Come" Preached July 22, 1984. Bethlehem Baptist Church. Part of a sermon series called *Ruth: Sweet and Bitter Providence*. http://www.desiringgod.org/resource-library/sermons/ruth-the-best-is-yet-to-come.

20. Bob Benson, *See You at the House* (Nashville: Generoux Nelson, 1989), 170.